THOUGHTS, MEMORIES
AND TEARS

Joye Enterprise • Palo Alto, California

DEDICATION
"TO THOSE WHOSE THOUGHTS AND MEMORIES STILL CAUSE THE TEARS TO FALL."

IN LOVING MEMORY OF COMBAT PARATROOPERS:

DALE F. YEE
AND
JOHN T. GRIFFIN

THEIR PURPLE HEARTS STILL PUMP FREEDOM THROUGH OUR NATION'S VEINS,
THEY SACRIFICED FOR OUR COUNTRY'S GAIN...
HONORABLE SUFFERINGS, NEVER IN VAIN,
NOW AND FOREVER, THEY SHARE OUR SAVIOR'S HEAVENLY DOMAIN...

Thoughts, Memories and Tears
by Peter S. Griffin

Copyrights Pending
Text and Photographs by Peter S. Griffin
Design and Artwork by Joye Enterprise

Poetry by Peter S. Griffin
Design and Compilation by Challen K. Yee
Associate Editor: Brenda G. Griffin
Photographer: Maxine Gibson

Manufactured in the United States of America

ISBN 0-9674049-0-8

FIRST PRINTING 1999

CONTENTS

Thoughts, Memories and Tears

Photo: The 187th Airborne Regimental Combat Team (ARCT) in a mass assault at Munsan-ni, Korea, Friday 23 March 1951. The attack caught the enemy completely by surprise and disrupted their retreat to the north. There were 3,300 U.S. Army paratroopers against 20,000 Chinese troops.

Cover: "Angel watching over paratroopers" Drawing by Challen K. Yee for the Dale Yee Memorial Back cover: Peter S. Griffin - Vietnam 1966.

by Peter S. Griffin

author, age 6

PHOTOGRAPHS • 60

MEMORIES • 72

TEARS • 113

"Grif" / Photo taken in Phan Rang, South Vietnam – May 1966

THOUGHTS, MEMORIES AND TEARS

The poems contained in these pages are an odyssey of heart and mind. They were written solely for enlightenment, not for recognition or profit. All were written in a therapeutic attempt to better understand life, death, war and surviving.

The human mind and heart are complex, indeed. I do not profess to be an authority in psychology or sociology. I'm simply trying to better understand behaviors resulting from traumatic experiences. This anthology is an attempt to accomplish that end.

War affects all participants in so many profound ways. It has a great impact on how one interprets his world. It affects how great one thinks, works, plays, worships, loves and behaves. It affects virtually every aspect of human life for the survivor.

It would be impossible to express all the feelings of a combat soldier or war survivor. Likewise to describe the many things they have seen and experienced. It is enough to say that war and its horrors are not easily forgotten. Its scars are deep and its wounds are not easily healed.

War should never be glorified. It causes damage so significant it staggers the imagination. In all cases, it causes irreparable harm, not only to man, but to every aspect of his world. Its survivors are never left as they once were. The losses of life and its sufferings are immeasurable.

Unfortunately, war can not always be avoided. We must pray for our leaders and all heads of governments, that they strive for peace in our world. If only we would obey God's commandments and live in harmony, as He directs.

When war is unavoidable, countries should not blame their soldiers. War and its many horrors result from flawed politics and failed diplomacy. It is not caused by protectors of the peace. Always support your soldiers, they are truly "America's native sons."

War is a circumstance beyond the common soldier's control. All soldiers provide national defense and will lay down their lives for their God, family, friends, and country. Do not despise them for their duties and beliefs.

Gold Star Parents should always be honored. They would lay down their lives gladly, if only their child, their soldier, could survive. They too, made a supreme sacrifice.

I firmly believe we should remember, always, those who lost their life to battle. They truly did lay down their life for their friends.

Please pray for the survivors of war, the civilian victims, the veterans and most of all, the children, the poor children. "Life became their nightmare, never to outgrow!"

After many THOUGHTS, MEMORIES, AND TEARS, I hope all of us find a better tomorrow. It is my most fervent wish that this publication helps all of us better understand war and its terrible consequences. God bless you all, peace be with you, always.

Most Sincerely,
Peter S. Griffin
"Grif"

BROTHERS THREE

Peter S. Griffin (Grif) was born 14 November 1946 in Oswego, New York. He joined the U.S. Army on 13 March 1964 and was honorably discharged on 10 March 1967. His unit assignments were Co. A, 2/502nd Infantry, 101st Airborne Division and Co. C, 2/505th Infantry, 82nd Airborne Division. On Memorial Day weekend, 1998, he was inducted into the 502nd Infantry Distinguished Members of the Regiment, Halls of Fame, in a ceremony at Ft. Campbell, Kentucky.

He is a "Boat Person", arriving in Viet Nam on 29 July 1965 aboard the "U.S.N.S. GENERAL LEROY ELTINGE". The 1st Brigade of the 101st Airborne operated separately until 1968, when the rest of the division arrived.

After discharge he attended the Police Academy at Syracuse, New York and served as a Police Officer in Oswego, New York from 1968 - 78. He also attended the State University College at Oswego, taking Public Justice courses.

His military decorations include, the Viet Nam Service Medal with two bronze battle stars, the Silver Star, the Army Commendation Medal, the Good Conduct Medal, the Republic of Viet Nam Campaign Medal with device (1960), the Republic of Viet Nam Cross of Gallantry with Palm, the Presidential Unit Citation with Oak Leaf Cluster, the Valorous Unit Citation, the Meritorious Unit Citation, the Parachute Badge, the Vietnamese Paratrooper Badge, the Combat Infantryman Badge, the Recondo Patch, the National Defense Service Medal and the Expert Rifleman Badge.

"Grif" married Brenda Gibson in 1967. They are blessed with daughter Pamela, and son Brent. They are the proud grandparents of three lovely granddaughters, Emilie, Meaghan and Georgia. They have resided in North Carolina for the past twenty-two years.

Two of Grif's brothers, John and William, also served in the Airborne:

Corporal **John T. Griffin** was killed in action, after parachuting behind enemy lines at Munsan-ni, Korea, on 25 March 1951. He was a member of Co. G, 2/187th Airborne Regimental Combat Team and was highly decorated. He also served in the U.S. Navy during World War II.

Brother **William J. Griffin Jr.** was a member of Co. A, 1/188th Airborne Infantry Regiment, 11th Airborne Division. He was an "Atomic Vet", having participated in "Operation Buster/Jangle" in October-November, 1951. They were the first troops to participate in the test of an atomic bomb. He is also deceased.

POST TRAUMATIC STRESS DISORDER

PTSD, COMBAT VETERANS WILL CARRY IT TO THEIR GRAVE,

BE SMART, GET HELP, REFUSE TO BECOME ITS SLAVE...

YOU MUST LEARN TO CONTROL ITS RAGE!

NEVER LET IT DICTATE, HOW YOU WILL BEHAVE...

DRUGS AND ALCOHOL, THE DEVIL'S TOOLS,

AVOID THIS HELL, DON'T BE SATAN'S FOOL..!

FOR THEN, YOUR GUILT WILL TURN TO SHAME...

YOUR GALLANT EFFORTS AND GOOD NAME,

DON'T DESERVE THAT TERRIBLE, EVIL,

SELF INFLICTED PAIN...

THEN, YOUR BURDEN, SURELY, BE TOO GREAT...

NOW, NO LONGER IN CONTROL OF YOUR FATE,

WEIGHTED AND LABELED, BY THAT DECEITFUL SNAKE ... !

POST-TRAUMATIC STRESS DISORDER
By
Pamela Anne Griffin Law, CBIS, CI-CE, CCC-SLP*

This article is revised slightly from its presentation in the 10th edition of Airborne Quarterly published in the Spring of 1997. The author wishes to share the contents of the article again with combat veterans as they connect with the thoughts, memories and tears in an attempt to find a better understanding of life, death, war and survival found in this book. I wish you God's speed as you connect with personal meaning to the pages found here and as you continue to live your life with courage and conviction. Most Respectfully, Pam.

Post-Traumatic Stress Disorder (PTSD) is the result of a psychologically distressing event that at the time of trauma produces fear, terror and helplessness because the trauma represents a threat to the survivor's or family member's life (APA, p. 247). I will attempt to synthesize factual information about PTSD while coloring it with knowledge I have gained as a result of my family's reaction to PTSD.

My father is a Vietnam Veteran who has been haunted by dead soldiers, his fallen comrades in arms for as long as I have been alive. A diagnosis of PTSD was not made until I was in my early 20's. My father's diagnosis helped me to see similar symptoms in myself that were the result of a motor vehicle accident in which I was critically injured, sustaining a Traumatic Brain Injury (TBI) and multiple other traumatic injuries some five years prior. I sought medical help to manage my reaction to the devastating trauma. I consider both situations to be cumulative traumas - the threat to life and the overwhelming fear resulted from continual and repeated exposure to devastating circumstances.

Current television and media exploration of PTSD have increased and can be seen in prime time television and in local news footage. An increased focus on PTSD has been seen in my own community in response to the Columbine High School shootings. However, veterans whose family and friends may be unaware of PTSD and its devastating effects on health and happiness, may be unfamiliar with its hallmarks. It is my hope that the information that follows will help readers who may or do suffer from PTSD to seek help if they have not. Family members may share this article with their loved one in the hopes of putting a name to what has become a part of the family's daily life. I hope to offer some new in-sights from PTSD experts that may be of benefit in mastering your trauma.

The Diagnostic and Statistical Manual of the American Psychiatric Association (1987) outlines the following criteria for a diagnosis of PTSD if they persist for at least one month:

> 1. Person experiences extreme trauma (i.e., combat veterans, accident survivors and victims of violence).

> 2. Person re-experiences the trauma through thoughts, dreams or flashbacks and/or has psychological distress when presented with triggers or psychological reminders of the trauma (i.e. anniversaries, gun shots, and disturbing news stories).

3. Person has avoidance of these triggers or feels numbness regarding their situation. This avoidance can be manifested in an inability to recall important aspects of the trauma, diminished interest in previously enjoyed activities, detachment from others or from one's own feelings and a sense of a foreshortened future.

4. Person has persistent increased arousal as evidenced by hypervigilance (continually on guard to ward off reoccurrence of trauma), poor sleep, irritability, poor concentration, exaggerated startle response and/or physiologic changes such as sweating when faced with a trigger.

The above symptoms can coexist with depression, anxiety, survivor guilt, emotional lability, self defeating behaviors, suicidal ideation, edginess or nervousness, anhedonia (inability to feel pleasure), drug or alcohol abuse or changes in cognitive functioning (reduced recall or poor concentration). (APA and Goleman).

According to Daniel Goleman, author of Emotional Intelligence, there is hope for those of us who suffer from PTSD. Goleman hypothesizes that PTSD survivors can relearn a more normal response to trauma by using role-playing, art (drawing/poetry), relaxation techniques or daydreams to recall and rethink our ordeals as a part of supportive psychotherapy. He believes we can enable ourselves to use our brain's frontal cortex to inhibit the amygdala, the portion of our brain which houses the stress-induced brain changes that are the result of the uncontrollable stressor which left us feeling overwhelmingly helpless and forms the foundation of PTSD.

Goleman cites the work of Harvard Psychiatrist, Judith Lewis Herman who outlines three stages in the lifelong recovery process of trauma recovery. Hermann identifies attaining a sense of safety, remembering the details of the trauma and mourning the loss it has brought and resumption of a normal life as indications of trauma mastery. Signs of trauma mastery can include strong, trusting relationships, control over emotional outbursts, changes in self-defeating responses, less distress when recalling the trauma and a reduction in anger, guilt and tension. I believe that trauma mastery is, like everything else, a work in progress. Progress for me is found in attempting to live life to the fullest, each and every day and facing my fears with faith, courage and conviction.

If you have already been diagnosed with PTSD, I encourage you to readily discuss concerns with your treating physician and/or your therapist. There are numerous medications available that may be beneficial to you. Some psychotherapy techniques include individual and group treatment, peer support groups, hypnosis and eye movement desensitization and reprocessing. Techniques used by a given therapist vary and some techniques have limited scientific support. Don't be afraid to ask your treating physician about available techniques. Contact your physician for information regarding medication, alternative medicine approaches or any of the mentioned psychotherapy techniques. A helpful solution that my Dad has found is poetry. He has authored numerous poems that reflect his recollections and response to PTSD. This article is intended to be a companion to the stories found in the following pages.

I have chosen to immerse myself in readings for trauma survivors and utilize journal writings and meditation to assist in nurturing my sense of self and to minimize the impact of my trauma on my life. I have come to recognize that I will never forget the date of my accident and many of the events, which unfolded, in my recovery. I recognize that I will cry when I hear of the untimely death of another teenager (especially seventeen year olds - my age at the time of the accident) or when I see individuals triumph over their adverse circumstances. I have also learned that this is OK - I am happier and stronger because of those tears.

I am grateful for my life and my recovery. I wish to give back my life in service to others and have chosen to pursue a doctoral degree in psychology so I can work with other trauma survivors attempting to master individual and often, cumulative traumas. Since the original presentation of this article, I have participated in acupuncture and herbal treatments to manage chronic physical pain resulting from my accident. Acupuncture has allowed me to exercise again, which in turn brightens my spirit. I encourage others to consider consultation with a qualified acupuncturist to see if there is an alternative management for you, too.

I have been blessed with a loving family and friends who enrich my life on a daily basis and for which I am truly grateful. It is my hope your family and friends can journey this life with you with loving encouragement and inspiration. I also hope that if you need help, you will seek the help of your local Veterans Administration Hospital, family physician, your fellow veterans and your family.

God Bless you for your service to our dear country and in your journey towards trauma mastery. I thank each of you in my prayers for the freedoms I enjoy. Always remember that your country owes you a debt of gratitude and even if citizens are unable to express it, they feel grateful, too. May God bless you in your journey towards trauma mastery.

Bibliography

American Psychiatric Association (1987). <u>Diagnostic and Statistical Manual of Mental Disorders Revised</u>, 3rd Edition Washington, DC: APA.

Goleman, D. (1995). <u>Emotional Intelligence</u>. NY: Bantam Books.

Reid, W.H., G.U. Ballis, & B.J. Sutton. (1997). <u>The Treatment of -Psychiatric Disorders, 3rd Edition, Revised for DSM IV</u>. Bristol, PA: Brunner/Mazel Publishers.

Author's Biographical Sketch

The author is a Certified Brain Injury Specialist, certified by the American Academy of Certification for Brain Injury Specialists (AACBIS). She is also certified as an AACBIS Clinical Instructor and Clinical Examiner. She holds a Certificate of Clinical Competence as a Speech-Language Pathologist from the American Speech-Language Hearing Association (ASHA). Her employment has spanned across the entire brain injury continuum of care.

She is currently employed as the Brain Injury Project Coordinator in a contracted position through the Colorado Department of Human Services, Office of Health and Rehabilitation and the Brain Injury Association of Colorado. She is enrolled as a concurrent master's/doctoral student in Psychology at California Coast University. CCU is a distance learning program based in Santa Ana, California.

She is married to Tucker Law and they have two daughters, Emilie and Meaghan. The family resides in Westminster, Colorado.

THE DEGREE OF SEVERITY

by
Peter S. Griffin

Volumes have been written on the symptoms, diagnoses and treatment of Post Traumatic Stress Disorder (PTSD) affecting the combat soldier. There is little a lay person could add to these professional and accurate conclusions.

I would, however, like to discuss the most devastating part of PTSD, THE DEGREE OF SEVERITY, which can ultimately destroy the life of the combat veteran. This point of view is my individual opinion only, based on personal experience as a PTSD victim and my observations of others suffering from PTSD.

It is my belief that basically there are only five criteria which influence the occurrence and severity of PTSD in the individual combat veteran. The degree of individual involvement in these categories directly effect the severity of the condition.

1) **DEDICATION** - the degree of risk, commitment and effort put forth by the individual in combat.

2) **EXPOSURE** - the degree and frequency of individual intense combat experienced.

3) **LOSS** - the degree of sufferings incurred, inflicted, or witnessed by the individual in combat.

4) **GUILT** - individual beliefs that what one did or failed to do, negatively effected the lives of others.

5) **BETRAYAL** - actual or perceived by the individual - committed by comrades, superiors, citizens or government that affected the outcome of the conflict.

The cumulative, detrimental effects of any combination of these criteria, will ultimately lead to the undoing of the sufferer. PTSD WILL, without doubt, destroy the individual's value of life or life itself. If you have PTSD symptoms do not deny them. Do not compound your problems by using illegal drugs or alcohol. They will offer no relief and will only add to your sufferings.

There is little hope for a meaningful life for those who remain undiagnosed and/or untreated. Therefore, I urge all who suffer from the symptoms of PTSD to seek professional medical assistance as soon as possible. Always remember, PTSD is an honorable condition resulting from your defense of our country and our way of life. Thank you for sacrificing for the freedoms we so enjoy everyday. God bless you and God bless America.

I SEEN YOU

I remember, I remember .... walking off that hill at Dak To, a mere lad of nineteen. I SEEN YOU there, Jim, you were walking at my side. You were covered in blood, the blood of your enemies, the blood of your fallen comrades, it was intermixed with that of your own. No longer was there the glint of youth in your eyes, it was replaced with a somber, empty stare. You said nothing as we walked, there was nothing you could say. You didn't need to utter a word, the hell we barely escaped was still dictating and rolling through our minds.... In this numbed state of mind, one thing and one thing only, did we realize..., that we were forever and irrevocably, changed. The innocence of our young lives was killed, it had died with so many of our fellow soldiers on those jungle covered hills surrounding the Dak Tan Kan Valley.

We had survived, we fought many fierce battles over the past twelve months, but this one, this one, was by far the bloodiest. The carnage, horror and death was incalculable in our young minds. We were stunned, but we were alive, and we had been victorious. We had put in our year. We were going home! To the Land Of The Big PX! We would be able to buy and enjoy whatever our pocketbooks would permit. Our tour was up and the nightmares behind us. We would be able to go and do as we pleased, no more fighting, suffering and dying. Or so we tried to tell ourselves.

Inside we really knew that things would never be the same. We realized that, when we walked off that hill. But still, we didn't want to admit it. There was no way we could predict the unrest and chaos that awaited us in the streets of our hometowns and in our minds.

> There was no way we could predict the unrest and chaos that awaited us in the streets of our hometowns and in our minds...

We were welcomed home, quietly and individually, by close friends and family. We didn't expect any fanfare nor did we get any. We melted into our civilian roles and jobs, as best we could. We watched the war and protests over the television and in our downtowns. There was little we could do as this unrest and division slowly broke our hearts. We watched Saigon fall, we watched the "boat people" as they tried to make their escapes, and we watched the killing fields spread throughout Laos and Cambodia.

No longer did we belong to our great society. We felt isolated and alone. We tucked the war inside us, as neatly as we could. We kept our feelings and experiences to ourselves, only sharing them with a trusted few. Slowly, ever so slowly, did we come to realize the severe damage this war had inflicted on the soul of our nation and to ourselves.

> We felt isolated and alone...

Many of us went for years without knowing what was eating at us from inside the depths of our minds. We suffered silently with flashbacks, nightmares, and intrusive thoughts. These problems invaded every aspect of our lives, inhibiting our personal relationships and subjecting many of us to the singular world of isolation. Many found that they were no longer in control of their emotions. They felt incapable of giving or receiving the love they so desperately needed.

Many suffer from guilt resulting from what they believe they did or failed to do. Alcohol and drug abuse took their toll on many of our veterans. To this very day there are many, many veterans out there suffering from Post Traumatic Stress Disorder that have not been diagnosed or treated for this very serious problem. PTSD has taken and ruined many lives over history. It is as old as war itself and in many ways, more cunning and ruthless than the most deliberate of enemies.

If there is only one thing to be stressed to our veterans about PTSD it is that it's an HONORABLE condition. They suffer from it as a result of fighting for their country. It knows no race, creed, color or rank. It is indiscriminating. Its only criteria is that you spent enough personal time in the hell of combat to meet its prerequisites.

Now, three decades later, I am coming out of my shell and into the light of reality. I have been diagnosed with PTSD and I am receiving proper treatment. I now know what's been wrong with me and I'm starting to feel much better. So good in fact, I think I'll go to my outfits' reunion. Perhaps I'll recognize some old buddies that I fought with and find out I'm not really alone, that there are others who share my feelings and understand what I've been through.

Jim, is that you I see sitting across the table from me? It is you, you staring into space. You, yes, you, with "The Thousand Yard Stare". I remember, I remember .... I SEEN YOU in action at the artillery site, as you were overrun at your listening post, as the enemy chased you back to the perimeter. I SEEN YOU throw grenades and empty the magazines in your rifle as the enemy blew their whistles and bugles in an all out charge. Yes, I remember, I SEEN YOU take a round and administer aid to the more seriously wounded soldiers. Have you been diagnosed with PTSD? You haven't? Lets walk down the hill together, again. This time we'll go to the nearest Veterans Administration Hospital, then we'll go to that Big PX. Yes, yes, it does seem like only yesterday, doesn't it?

...it is ... an HONORABLE condition

THOUGHTS

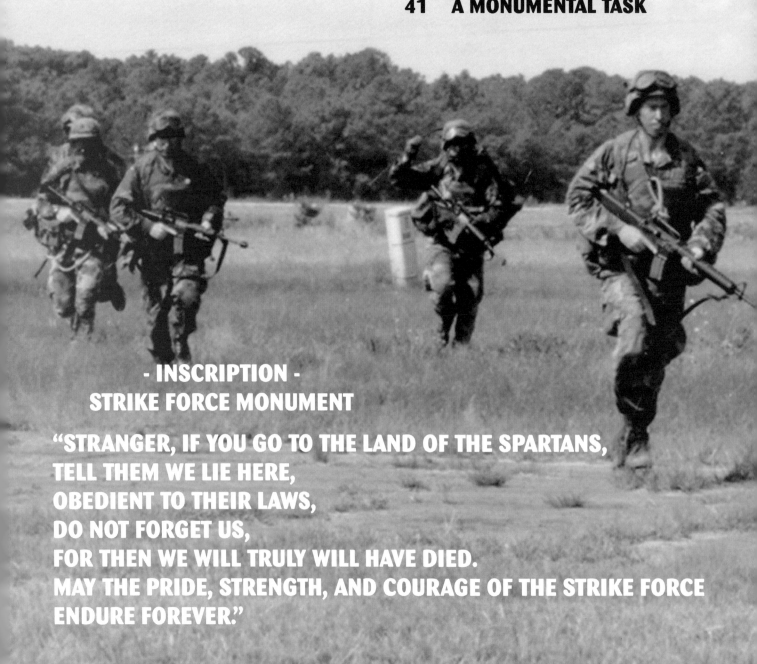

- INSCRIPTION -
STRIKE FORCE MONUMENT

"STRANGER, IF YOU GO TO THE LAND OF THE SPARTANS,
TELL THEM WE LIE HERE,
OBEDIENT TO THEIR LAWS,
DO NOT FORGET US,
FOR THEN WE WILL TRULY WILL HAVE DIED.
MAY THE PRIDE, STRENGTH, AND COURAGE OF THE STRIKE FORCE
ENDURE FOREVER."

MEDAL OF HONOR

DALE E. WAYRYNEN   18 MAY 1967
MILTON A. LEE   26 APRIL 1968
FRANK R. FRATELLENIC0   19 AUGUST 1970

AT LEAST 448 2/502 SOLDIERS WERE KILLED IN VIETNAM AND AT LEAST 2500 WERE WOUNDED. NEARLY EVERY MAN COMMITTED TO THE RIFLE PLATOONS OF THE BATTALION BECAME A COMBAT CASUALTY.

A VETERAN'S ODYSSEY

To be young, able, and willing,
The thought of war, oh so thrilling....
To meet the test, to be the best,
To earn the right, to join the quest....

To wear the uniform, to take up arms,
To protect your country from all harm....
To shoulder a weapon, to take aim,
To take the risk for mankind's gain.....

Hatred, anger is not the measure,
To serve country is your pleasure....
The honor is yours, instilled in training,
Unit pride will be your guide....

So excited to arrive,
Never doubting you'll survive....
Look around, take a survey,
All the soldiers in such a hurry....

Saddle up, move it out,
Engage the enemy in a rout....
To beat the enemy at his game,
Destroying him will be your fame....

It's so hot, the jungle thick,
Insects and animals, oh so quick....
Look out for mines and booby traps,
If you fail, you'll breathe your last.....

Spider holes in bamboo groves,
Fire ants that attack in droves...
Scan the trees, look for snipers,
Elephant grass full of vipers.....

All your senses are so keen,
What in the hell caused that scream...
Look around, hear that sound,
Charlie's hiding in the ground.....

Machine guns crack, mortars blast,
Fellow soldiers taking flak....
Whistles blow, blood will flow,
Enemy tracers on the glow.....

Open up, fire at will,
Cover your flank, take that hill...
Bullets flying, men are dying,
Show no fear, cover your rear.....

Pop the smoke, this ain't no joke,
"Willie Peter" bursting in air.....
Burning flesh on the tear,
How in the hell will I make a year...

Helmets gone and ammo's low,
Claymores in trees, ain't no breeze....
Rockets pound, one hell of a sound,
All my buddies taking rounds.....

Gather your wounded and regroup,
Where in the hell's the rest of the troop..?
"Snake and nape" in the air,
Enemy soldiers everywhere....

Hunker down, hug the ground,
"Smokey the Bear" is in the air...
Fire power so immense,
Enemy attack still intense.....

Radios, all are cracking,
Friendly units are attacking.....
Choppers soar, the battle roars,
Ain't no doubt, this is war....

Charlie runs but he can't hide,
Taking bullets from all sides....
One last effort, all in vain,
Never have I seen such pain.....

To catch the enemy in my sight,
To shoot for what you believe is right....
To see him fall and groan in pain,
Later wondering what was his name...?

Was he loved, will he be missed,
Had he a wife he loved to kiss....?
Perhaps some children bear his name,
Later to play the killing game....

All is quiet, it begins to rain,
I wonder if I'm still the same....
The dreaded looks, on all those faces,
Empty eyes, grotesque places....

It's all over, they say we won,
Wonder how, it all begun....
I look around, my friends are gone,
I wonder if I still belong....

A year's gone by, it's time to go, I did my best,
The orders given, dress right dress...
I wonder where, are all the rest,
Soldiers missing, oh so less.......

Years go by, I think I've made
But inside, I just can't fake...
Feelings are so suppressed,
Why can't I be like the rest....

War never leaves, forever gone,
Death leaves people most forlorn...
Decades pass, but still it lasts,
Still perpetuating its evil past....

Perhaps some day when we awake
We'll finally kill that evil snake...
Satan must surely pay,
For what he does, his evil ways....

Happiness does abound,
But it stops when I'm around...
Often I just stare in space,
Wonder why, I'm out of place...?

No matter what I try to do,
Just can't stop and think it through...
Memories keep flooding back,
Men are dying in attack.....

Seems so real, wish I'd heal,
It's so sad, to be alone...
No one to talk to, no one home,
Living life, as if a drone.....

Preservation demands isolation,
Deeply hampering all relations...
Try to fight with all my might,
Trying to make my life seem right....

Wish I knew, what went wrong,
Want so much to belong...
Friends and loved ones, really care,
Want so much, my life to share.....

With God's help I have no fear,
Happiness will reappear....
It is right to remember,
But everyday... the devil's embers...!

Charlie:Viet Cong   "Willie Peter":White phosphorous ammunition   Claymores: Anti-personnel mines
     "Snake and nape": Aerial bombs/ napalm   "Smokey the Bear": C-47 aircraft-(flareship)

ANGELS AND EAGLES

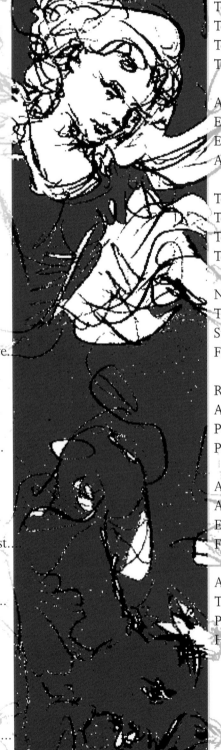

Angels protect and defend,
What is sacred to the end....
Always fighting to amend,
Evil acts destroying men....

Angels guard Heaven's gate,
They pull patrols to ensure our fate ....
Devil's and demons quake in fear,
When and where ever angels appear....

Evil lurks all over our sphere,
Creating chaos and spreading fear...
Thus the reasons angels enlist,
Courageous soldiers for an assist ....

Eagles, those who are true of heart,
The angels earthly counterparts....
Eagles, proud and brave,
Soldiers who fight, in spite of the grave.

To join the angels in their fight,
To aid the oppressed in their plight ....
To right the wrongs, of evil doing,
To kill the seeds before their spewing...

To STRIKE the devil, hard and fast,
To MAKE HIS PAIN, FOREVER LAST....
To make him curse, his evil past,
To make him suffer and breathe his last...

To promote health and healing,
To give to men, the right of kneeling....
To pray to God, sincere in feeling,
To thank him for, their very being....

Angels and Eagles, joined together,
Forming a bond that lasts forever....
Angels and Eagles who fight and toil,
Protecting God's most precious spoils....

To pick up the sword, to take the risk,
To spread their wings, to make a fist....
To STRIKE a blow, for what is right,
To give their lives for mankind's strife....

Angels and Eagles, surely the best
Engaged in God's most holy quest....
Evil's battles will lose their zest,
Angels and Eagles, ABOVE THE REST....

To make our world, a better place,
To spread to all, God's saving grace....
To put a smile on his face,
To see his warriors interlaced. ..!

Nothing less can make God cry,
The precious loss, of his allies....
Still they fight and will preserve,
Freedom's song of heavenly words....

Righteousness will prevail,
Angels and Eagles, will not fail....
Peace on earth, is their goal,
Protecting lives and saving souls....

Angels and Eagles, both AIRBORNE,
All God's enemies, be forewarned...!
Evil will most surely die,
From attack, from on high...!

Angels and Eagles, SECOND TO NONE,
The glorious day, all wars are won. . . .
Perhaps that day, for what they've done,
HEAVEN AND EARTH, WILL BE AS ONE....

"OLD ABE"

Enemy beware when OLD ABE is near,
A predator of flight, by day or by night,
The eagle will strike with a terrible might....
His feathers are made of soldiers of nether,
They will send you to hell, no matter the weather....

They will appear from out of nowhere,
And death you will fear, for it is so near....
You shall run for cover when he hovers,
Too soon to discover,
the shadow of death you have just met....

His eyes are keen and he has seen,
The fear of death that you have left....
Your body trembles as he assembles,
Too late you know, there's nowhere to go....

His talons are sharp, as they cut you apart,
Your screams you shall hear as Hades grows near...
The devil, you say, is on his way,
To collect his pay, on your dying day....

Your escape is marred as he strikes hard,
It is over fast as you breathe your last...
But before you go, you have come to know,
Exactly what, I TOLD YOU SO...!

WAKE UP, AMERICA !

Symbolic attacks should warn us you know,
Reality sets in where fear begins...
America's enemies will strike anywhere,
They will do anything to instill that fear...

To put you on edge to walk on the ledge,
To see yourself fall, innocence mauled...
Shock effect will take its toll,
Destroying us is their goal...

Wake up America before it's too late,
Don't let terrorists seal our fate...
Our indecisions and lack of resolve,
Feeds their ambitions,
they have no prohibitions ...

To kill many birds with one stone,
To turn our congregations into war zones...
The destruction of our institutions,
Strengthen their resolutions...

To instill terror whatever the cost,
Their desired effect no matter our loss...
The more damage done,
the more they have won,
To kill our children is to destroy our future...

In their minds, terror has no errors,
A desired effect they can select...
The holiest place is no disgrace,
The safest place the greater the waste...

Multiple targets in one location,
Penetration will rattle our nation...
No place safe no matter our race,
To destroy us all is their call...

Psychological damage is their tool,
Cunning demons, they are not fools...
To weaken us within to our chagrin,
Their victory begins when morale caves in....

They know our weakness,
They know our plight....
Class distinction, racial strife, discrimination,
All will lead to our elimination...!

Let us learn from our mistakes,
Obsession with pleasure is a disgrace...
"One Nation under God " is the call,
If we live by this we will not fall....

Teach our children, right from wrong,
Preserve tranquility, support our military...
Following God is where we belong,
With Him on our side we can't go wrong....

Support our leaders, pray to God,
This is not a faraway war; it's on our sod...
Join together, so we are great,
Wake up America before it's too late...

AIRBORNE TOAST

Airborne soldiers, pride of the sky,
Fighting soldiers who never say die,
Over fifty years since our birth,
Over fifty years of proven worth,
Decisive victories are no mystery,
Defeating enemies are our history,
Enemy beware when we are near,
We are ready, we know no fear,
When you least expect us, we are there,
We travel light, we arrive by flight,
Certain death will be your plight,
Airborne soldiers of the past,
Valorous deeds that surely last,
Troopers of WWII,
Left a legacy to pursue,
Troopers of Korean Vintage,
Fought like hell to the finish,

Troopers of Viet Nam,
Fought in jungles of napalm,
Troopers of Desert Storm,
Left Saddam most forlorn,
Present troopers highly trained,
Our proud tradition, they retain,
Future troopers will be molded,
Our fighting spirit, never eroded,
Enemy know, we are locked and loaded,
Our fallen brothers who were slain,
Be it known, their spirit remains
An Airborne death is never in vain,
God and country eases our pain,
Our fallen brothers we salute,
Your sacrifice, most acute,
Rest in peace, and be assured,
Your precious memory be preserved.

THE AIRBORNE WALK
A TRIBUTE TO EVERY PERSON WHO HAS
BEEN OR WILL BE AIRBORNE QUALIFIED.
DEDICATED
APRIL 17, 1986

BY
SECRETARY OF THE ARMY
JOHN O. MARSH, JR.

TOLERANCE OF THE SHOAH
TO THE PEOPLE OF THE WORLD

What is knowledge, just what does it say,
Wisdom is knowledge, fear of Yahweh.....
Truth and righteousness, is the blend,
They form wisdom, our desired friend.....

If wisdom is the desired goal,
How on earth can we ignore the Shoah?
Ethnic cleansing is its means,
How can we ignore the screams?

What on earth is worth dying for?
Slavery is a word we all abhor!
A holocaust is not its metaphor,
Its consequences are much more!

To destroy a race, to call it purification,
Is this not evil's subrogation?
Is this not "Beezlebub's" ultimate weapon?
Wrong will permeate every nation!

Are we all, not one upon the earth?
A Shoah must be stopped, before its birth.....
If one should rear its ugly head,
A force of arms, must be led.....

War is justified response, to this hell on earth,
Righteousness must prove its worth.....
Evil will not, just go away,
We must fight to light the way....

For we are a brotherhood of nations,
Evil must be defeated, in our relations....
For all of us, to get along,
Our convictions must be strong!

The whole world is our community,
We must preserve human dignity....
We must stop the holocaust, where it begins,
It must not matter, origin or region!

Jesus taught us, a most divine lesson,
We must interpret his direction....
Did he not die, in our subrogation?
A holocaust is hate's manifestation....

Where ever on earth, this should appear,
We must overlook, our personal fears.....
A Shoah is always under our nose,
We must not permit, our eyes to close!

Never forget, that YOU are next,
Evil will try to confuse and perplex.....
"Tolerance of the Shoah",
Will drown the descendants of Noah.....

What have we learned from the Jewish Holocaust?

God Bless our troops in Bosnia! --Grif

WAR...

WHAT IS IT GOOD FOR?

HOW MANY TIMES HAVE I HEARD IT BEFORE,
"WAR, WHAT IS IT GOOD FOR"....?
DON'T THESE PEOPLE UNDERSTAND,
FREEDOM'S THE LIFE BLOOD OF OUR LAND..

"OLD GLORY" STANDS FOR MANY THINGS,
MOST IMPORTANT, LETTING FREEDOM RING....
FREEDOM OF SPEECH IS A WONDERFUL THING,
BUT IF WRONGLY APPLIED,
OUR SOLDIERS DIE.....!

DON'T THESE PEOPLE UNDERSTAND,
WHEN EVIL STRIKES,
WE MUST TAKE A STAND.....
EVIL EMPIRES STILL PERSIST,
IF THEY CONQUER,
MANY HORRORS WILL EXIST.....

TO SUBDUE A RACE, TO DESTROY A FLAG,
TO CONQUER A PEOPLE, TO MAKE THEM BEG....
TO TAKE THEIR POSSESSIONS
AND THEIR LANDS,
TO RAVAGE THE WORK
OF THEIR CREATIVE HANDS....

TO CRUSH A PEACEFUL PEOPLE AND
THEIR DREAMS,
TO RAPE, TO PILLAGE,
TO MAKE THEM SCREAM.....
TO ENSLAVE AND MURDER,
INNOCENT HUMAN BEINGS,
TO TORTURE THE CHILDREN,
UNSPEAKABLE THINGS.....

BECAUSE SUCH HORRORS DO EXIST,
MANY BRAVE PEOPLE STILL ENLIST......
TO SERVE THEIR COUNTRY AND MANKIND,
TO PRESERVE FREEDOM AND PEACE OF MIND....

"WAR, WHAT IS IT GOOD FOR?"
WHEN COMMON SENSE AND TALKING FAIL....
WHEN DIPLOMATS ARE THROWN IN JAIL,
WHEN THE STRONG ABUSE THE FRAIL...

WHEN WRONG OVER POWERS RIGHT,
WHEN DICTATORS ABUSE THEIR MIGHT...
WHEN EVIL STALKS BOTH DAY AND NIGHT,
THANK GOD FOR WARRIORS,
UNAFRAID TO FIGHT.....!

SOMETIMES WAR IS A NECESSARY THING,
TO RESTORE DIGNITY
TO ALL HUMAN BEINGS......
TO PROTECT OUR PRECIOUS HUMAN RIGHTS,
TO HELP THE OPPRESSED, IN THEIR PLIGHT....!

SO I SAY, TO ALL WHO WONDER,
HOW ELSE, CAN WE STOP THE PLUNDER......?
WHEN EVIL FAILS TO LISTEN,
ONLY BRAVERY,
WILL PREVENT SUBMISSION......!

THE WORSE THING, YOU CAN DO,
TO TELL A SOLDIER, HE'S A FOOL...!
HE FOUGHT THE WAR, SO YOU'D BE FREE,
YOUR IGNORANCE,
MAY BRING YOU TO YOUR KNEES....!

NOW YOU KNOW, WHAT WAR IS GOOD FOR,
IT PROTECTS YOUR FREEDOMS
AND YOUR RIGHTS.....
YOU'RE THE FOOL,
TO CURSE THIS SAVING MIGHT,
THE BRAVE PEOPLE,
WHO PROTECT YOUR LIFE....!

THE WINDOW OF PEACE

Why does it take a major war,
Natural disasters, hardships galore....
For all of us to understand,
Living in harmony is God's plan....

Look at our history and you can see,
A window of peace and harmony....
In times of despair, we really cared,
Looking out for one another, throughout the years....

In the early days, of the pioneers,
Helping each other, the land was cleared .....
In times of drought, together, we fought,
Side by side, our neighbor's well, would provide...

When our country was at war,
Women and children, left to the chores ....
All our men, fought as one,
All of our enemies, were on the run .....

During the Depression, all lent a hand,
To eradicate starvation, from our land....
Pulling together, all along the way,
We rebuilt our economy, much better today....

Are we all too comfortable, now ... ?
Perhaps, not enough sweat, on the brow ... ?
For all of us to get along,
Our belief in God, must be strong...

Ethnicity, is our own racial composition and history,
Diversity should not be a reason for
disunity and bigotry....
All of us, should be very proud,
Our origins, should be, our foundation sound...

Indians, Blacks, Whites, no matter our hue,
Respecting each other, will bind us like glue ....
All of us, have so much to give,
Sharing our blessings, in joy, we could live ...

Treating each other, as if our child,
Our society, would not, run wild....
The color of skin, is not where hatred begins,
Coveting each other, our morals cave in... !

Why should any of us feel exiled?,
Helping each other, our anger, not riled....
The act of sharing, makes people caring,
The joy of giving, makes life worth living ...

All of us, have our limits,
Not always, can we afford to give it ....
So just a smile, or a kind word,
A helping hand, would bless our land ....

Look into the eyes, of someone in need,
You will see the window of opportunity....
For the eyes are the window of the soul,
Caring for each other, we'll achieve our goals....

All of us can lead a peaceful, bountiful life,
If only we act, to end our strife....
Even Jesus had to sacrifice!,
What an example, to live our lives....

Happiness is not effortless,
All of us can be so blessed....
If only we would show our best,
And treat our least, as if our guest...

We can achieve happiness, peace and harmony,
Just eliminate our hatreds and animosities ... !
By caring for each other, crime and war will cease,
All we need to do is, open THE WINDOW OF PEACE

————————

NO GREATER GIFT

What is the greatest thing, a person can do ?
Tis, to give their life, for the love of YOU.....
A soldier is this type of person,
He will suffer and die, your well being, the reason....

He will take on, near impossible tasks,
He will do what his country asks...
He does this for love of country and you,
Training day and night,
preparing for the vicious fight....

Going anywhere, in a moment's notice,
Fighting like hell, enemy attacks, he'll quell....
Striking hard, he'll give no quarter,
He stands between you and your slaughter....

Restoring peace to a troubled land,
He needs your support, back your country's plan....
Don't find fault, for the sake of criticism,
His duty is his CATECHISM...!

He's willing to shed his blood, to protect your life,
Your rush to judgment, cuts like a knife...!
When you protest the war, his heart is broken,
This undermines his fighting spirit,
his life may perish !

It's not his decision, where or who to fight,
He's responding to his government's plight....
THEY issue the orders, THEY have the plan,
The soldiers only goal, to protect our land....

Politics are not his to ponder,
He must obey orders and protect our borders....
It's not in his power to question authority,
Serving is where his duty lies,
IT IS HIS TO DO OR DIE ...!

What is right or what is wrong,
Debate does not make, our forces strong...!
ELECT leaders you can trust,
Eradicating doubt, a major plus... !

When it's time to take up arms,
Indecision, causes great harm....
To distract him from his mission,
Bleeding profusely, could become
his condition . . . !

Dangerous assignments,
they will successfully complete,
Your encouraging word, PREVENTS DEFEAT...!
When our military has been sent on a mission,
Your support and prayers,
vastly improves their condition...!

NO GREATER GIFT, could they give,
They'll give their life, so YOU can live....
Your freedom, peace and safety, is their goal,
NO GREATER GIFT could you give,
Your TOTAL SUPPORT for their role!!!!

"IT DON'T MEAN NOTHING"...!

To be young, strong, up to the test,
To join the military, to give your best....
Taught strong beliefs in patriotism,
Protecting flag and country, a noble decision....

A worthy cause may arise,
You train hard so you'll survive....
To defend our constitution, you'll answer the call,
America's promise, "Equality for all"....

To put yourself in harm's way,
To protect your country, you'll not sway....
If you must, you'll pay the toll,
You'll give your life, to save their souls....

The day does come, you get your orders,
Enemy soldiers have crossed the border...
Freedom is dying in a faraway land,
You'll serve in combat, in Viet Nam....

Different people, different cultures,
Difficult terrain, looming vultures....
Climate hot, meals are not,
Everything dirty, but the cause is worthy....

Monsoon rains, poisonous snakes,
Dysentery, diarrhea, belly aches....
Too much danger, too little sleep,
Tigers follow battles, much flesh to eat....

"IT DON'T MEAN NOTHING"...!

The enemy is smart, very cunning,
Tunnels in ground, difficult hunting....
Camouflaged to an art, he's out there, in the dark,
Finding and destroying him, will be no lark....

Friend by day, foe by night,
Guerrillas refuse to engage, in fair fights...
Snipers, ambushes, booby traps,
Despicable tactics, make them laugh....

Caches are hidden, bikes are ridden,
Supplies are stolen, feet are swollen....
Don't walk on dikes, stay off the paths,
If you don't, a sudden blast, soldiers breathe their last....

Hanoi Hanna is on the horn,
Her American guests talk, your heart is torn...
"The Peoples Army is the best,
U.S. Imperialists will die, like all the rest"...!

"IT DON'T MEAN NOTHING"....

Our troop strength is alarming,
Washington is not responding....!
Westmoreland asks for more,
Politicians refuse to back the war....

Our flag is burning, my stomach is churning,
Sick as hell, how death does smell....!
Jungle thick, mosquitoes quick,
Out of water, please just a lick?....

Leeches are finding, my body warmth,
All my fluids are pouring forth.....
Evacuation, in more ways than one,
My body trembling, head coming undone.....

Hospital is a tent, damn heat won't relent,
Fever won't give no quarter.....
Men in pain, all are lame,
Vision blurred, nothing to look at, just the same....

"IT DON'T MEAN NOTHING"

It's not long, back to war I go,
Battle after battle, the long war grows...
Seeing my friends blown to pieces,
Wading through rice paddies, human feces....

Hard core troops, from the north,
Well equipped, are pouring forth....
Major battles taking place,
Our South Vietnamese allies, losing faith...!

Victor Charlie is growing bold,
Russia's support and black market gold.....
Politicians back home, their support really waning,
Hippies on Capitol Hill,
Viet Cong Flags they're waving...!

"IT DON'T MEAN NOTHING"

Young people back home don't really care,
They're making love and growing hair.....
Preaching peace, deferments, just stay in school!
They hate authority, won't follow the rules.....

Smoking dope, skipping rope, making jokes,
Burning their draft cards and their bras.....
Drinking beer and playing cards,
Protesting all over the place, cops can't keep the pace....

Jane Fonda loves the Viet Cong and Tom Hayden,
A hippie leader, crude, unshaven....
Tis "The Age of Aquarius",
How they love their cannabis...!

Ho Chi Minh is mighty pleased,
Their peace movement is gaining speed.....
Every peace rally and demonstration,
Fills our enemy with great elation...!

"IT DON'T MEAN NOTHING"

All their protests have taken their toll,
U. S. policy has lost its goals.....
The fall of Saigon's greeted by cheers,
So many young soldiers, death's stolen their years....

Survivors,the veterans come home to despair,
Welcomed by ridicule animosity and jeers....
Struggling to find a place in society,
Many turn to drugs and alcohol lost sobriety ... !

Divorce, depression, suicide, disgrace,
In their own country, they're out of place....!
Their efforts, sacrifices, wounds and dreams,
No one listening, to hear their screams....!

What is their problem, are they just weak?
Deaf ears, refuse to hear them speak....
Second class citizens, it's all they are,
Not our problem, they're not up to par....!

Post traumatic stress disorder? Just an excuse!
Don't give a damn, if they're all recluse....
What happened in Viet Nam wasn't our fault!
The damn military, wouldn't stay the course....!

"IT DON'T MEAN NOTHING"

Many years have passed, opinion has swayed,
The public supports the military, nowadays....
Compassion is shown when they visit "The Wall",
Some even say "The soldiers stood tall!".....

Now the hippies are successful and rich,
Well educated, executives, they've found their niche....
Surrounded by material things, they claimed to hate,
Political correctness one hundred dollars a plate,
Hippie teachers slant the war,
depict soldiers evil, to the core....!

Luxury cars, beautiful homes, glamorous women
The social elite, the world's at their feet.....
Now they just enjoy Canada, from the ski towers,
The liberals in power, society's flowers....

They've cut the military down to size,
The protestors won the prize...
Don't worry, you hippies and yippies,
there will always be,
Brave young people, who really love our country....

Most raised by the poor, they'll go to war,
When it's all over, they can plant your flowers,
open your doors...
Don't feel guilty,
It wasn't your war!... or was it?

"IT DON'T MEAN NOTHING"!

A MOST DELICATE MISSION

Our forces given, A MOST DELICATE MISSION,
To restore peace, relieve Bosnia's condition....
Our military, doing what's right,
To transform, the dark of war, to peaceful light....

The American people, unsure of the cause,
Still harbour fears, of what Viet Nam was....
They must be shown, what they need to know,
The seeds of peace, need the chance to grow...

Our military, assigned, A MOST DELICATE MISSION,
We need to observe, care, and listen....
An uneasy peace, so hard to enforce,
They can do the job, let's help them stay the course...!

Blood spilled by hatred, runs so deep,
Only one year, no time to sleep....
Our soldiers must be alert, they must take care,
OUR total support, will lessen their fears...!

Many obstacles lay in their path,
With our help, THEY CAN, stop the blood bath...!!!!
The Bosnian people, so tired of war,
Will welcome peace, let's prop open the door...!!!!

Peaceful transitions, WE CAN negotiate,
Quick tempers, WE CAN conciliate...!
Unspeakable atrocities, have taken place,
They need our help and God's saving grace...!

Our encouragement, prayers, and support,
Sarajevo transformed, NO LONGER A FORT...!!!!
A MOST DELICATE MISSION is taking place,
To their children, WE CAN restore, a smiling face..!!!!

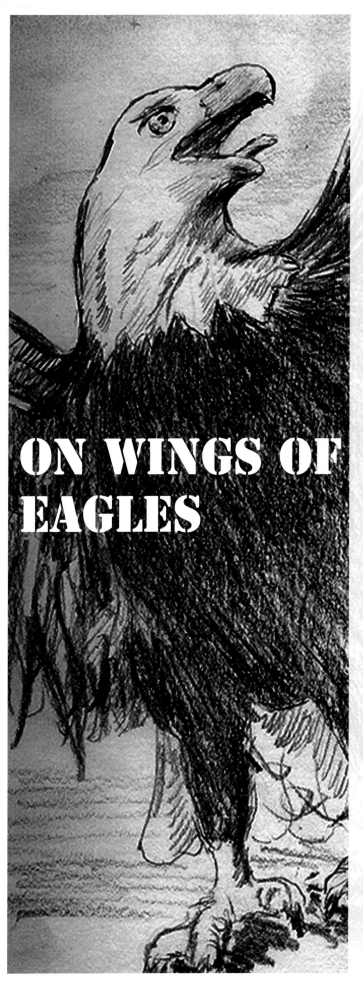

ON WINGS OF EAGLES

The Eagle soars through clear blue skies,
Keeping watch, over the peace that thrives....
Talons flexed, should a threat arise,
To challenge all enemies, no compromise....

Screaming Eagles, past, present, and future,
Lady Liberty will be protected and nurtured....
Elite soldiers, that protect and defend,
On Wings of Eagles, her promise depends....

Her torch of freedom, burns bright and great,
On Wings of Eagles, brave soldiers, protect her gates...
Eagle wings encompass her mighty division,
No enemy can alter, their objective or mission....

On Wings of Eagles, freedom's future lies,
If challenged, Airborne Soldiers, quick to rise...
On this fact, Lady Liberty, rests assured,
The rattling of sabers will be heard...!

Screaming Eagles ensure her plan,
Freedom rings throughout her land...
Mighty wings, will take to flight,
Bearing her soldiers, ready to fight....

On Wings of Eagles, gallant troopers, alertly perch,
Peace, they'll spread, throughout the earth....
Keen eyes will detect the birth,
Should evil empires, try to expand their girth....

On Wings of Eagles, victories will be repeated,
The defeat of evil, will be completed...
Cheers will fill the peaceful skies,
God's children, no longer, will suffer and die...!

Valor and bravery will set the stride,
Freedom's seeds will spread, far and wide....
On Wings of Eagles, liberty, so fast to grow,
From these wings, peace, be sowed....

On Wings of Eagles, America can rely,
Of history passed, and as time goes by....
Screaming Eagles, freedom's guardians, soar on high,
On Wings of Eagles,
Lady Liberty's freedom, will survive...!

"PEACE THROUGH STRENGTH"

DANCING WITH THE GRIM REAPER

The sounds of war, come crashing down,
Fast as lightning, death wears a frown...
Soldiers caught, in the Reaper's embrace,
Life's breath leaves, without a trace....

        Bombs explode, the cymbals clash,
        Machine guns roar, The Reaper laughs....
        The Devil's busy, collecting souls,
        War is hell, innocence pays the tolls....

The gates of hell are open wide,
The melody plays on, as soldiers die....
Dodging bullets, they stoop and sway,
The Reaper dances, he leads the way....

        They dig the earth, in which to hide,
        The Reaper's sickle, swings in stride....
        There's no escaping death, you see,
        The Reaper's dance, for you and me....

The crescendo heightens, as chaos reigns,
Cadence is kept, to the cries of pain....
The smell of death, vivid realization,
The wages of war, death and tribulation....

        To death's music, there is no harmony,
        Its notes, conceived of brutal agony....
        Grenades explode, life gets, still cheaper,
        Death so close,
        DANCING WITH THE GRIM REAPER....

The hounds of hell, are set free,
Snipers in trees, fill the balcony....
No one escapes his dance, it's personal, toe to toe,
Napalm explodes, illuminating, the darkest shadows....

        The skies open, as God sheds his tears,
        The Reaper keeps dancing, he has no fears....
        Death's now playing its saddest song,
        To its inventory, youth, now belong....

The sounds of death, keep a steady beat,
Even bravery and valor, suffer defeat.....
The rhythm of hell, plays on forever,
You'll find peace, on "The Twelfth of Never"...

        As the dance, slowly, comes to an end,
        Life leaves the body, as death settles in....
        Rigor-mortis has its profound, ugly, effect,
        In survivor's minds, it replays and reflects....

Decapitation, dismemberment, death so grotesque,
Crumpled bodies, loyalty's disfigurement....
Post Traumatic Stress Disorder, the Devil's sleeper,
You'll get little rest, DANCING WITH THE GRIM REAPER....!!!!

THE MARK OF CAIN

Fellow warriors, please listen clear,
The curse of war, may be, less severe...
We fought a war, provoked by man,
We tossed aside, God's most holy plan....

"Thou Shall Not Kill",
written by God's hand,
The passage of time, it does withstand....
Cain, the first, to cross the line,
He dared to anger, The Most Divine....

Exiled, for this serious mistake,
To bear God's mark, became his fate....
Not a mark, upon his head,
But state of mind, to be passed,
for the rest of time..

Meant for all of mankind to see,
Haunting him, till the soul, be free....
He killed—Man, God's most
precious creation,
Deprived his life, its blessed duration....

Some killings, justified by man,
Can't erase, Cain's deserved brand....
GUILT, you see, is THE MARK OF CAIN,
The rest of life, it will remain....

Guilt will permeate, your way of life,
It will agonize, both day and night...
Drugs and alcohol, the devil's tools,
Offer no peace, abused by fools....

Horrible nightmares, will end your sleep,
Invasive thoughts, in your mind,
will creep....
Self exile, becomes your retreat,
Mistrust of others, adds to defeat....

Though you killed, for reasons right,
Will not exclude, this terrible plight...
Death must come, from God alone,
Judgments of man, can't rule his throne....

The laws of man, never supersedes,
God will bring us, to our knees....
When blood is spilled, by our own hand,
Evil's chaos, will reign our land...!

The just and unjust, must bear this mark,
During life, will not depart....
For those who killed, for righteous sake,
Burning in hell, not be their Fate....

For when forced, to strike, a fatal blow,
Provocation may have come,
from hell below....
Righteous men, brave, they take a stand,
Peace will come, from Yahweh's lamb....

So my brothers, be contrite,
Pray, Christ will free you, from your plight....
Though you bear, THE MARK OF CAIN,
In God's Kingdom, you'll bear no blame...!

GHOSTS OF BATTLES PAST

Spirits of those, claimed in the fight,
Leave to us, to do what's right...
They gave their lives, for love of others,
They've become, our beloved brothers.....

They are, Ghosts of Battles Past,
In our hearts, their spirit lasts.....
They share with us, their special love,
Remember them, for what they've done......

The time of warriors, a fleeting thing,
Gabriel's trumpet calls, the Angels sing...
The souls of troopers, take to wing,
A soldier's death, how battle stings.....

Don't let their spirit roam,
In your heart, give them a home....
Their death then has, a sacred meaning,
Not in vain, their sacrifice, glowing, beaming....

To some, he's gone, eternity, he now belongs,
Quiet, listen, you'll hear his song.....
He's telling you, hold back those tears,
He'll be with you, throughout the years.....

Tragic events will stay in your mind,
Like sad movies, they play, then rewind....
Never ending, awake or asleep,
Just a reminder, their love to keep......

Death's anniversary, will come, then go,
It gives you the chance, their love to grow....
Refuse to let, their deaths be sad,
Celebrate their love, the love, you have....

A friend like him, never dies,
In your heart, his spirit thrives.....
He gives to you, that part of him,
His lasting love, you two, now kin.....

They stay with you, not to haunt or taunt,
Simply because, there's something they want...
Their desperate need, not to conceive guilt,
Just remember them, their spirit not wilt...

When you hear, the sound of "Taps",
That song of, Ghosts of Battles Past.....
T'is their bugle, pure and solemn,
Reminding you, one day, you join their column.....

Till then, rejoice, you know the secret,
In your heart, the locket, you keep it...
Death can't steal, this love that lasts,
Live on, be at peace, for Ghosts of Battles Past....!

This poem was inspired by Trooper Ed Beal. He served two tours in Vietnam, in the First Cavalry Division and the 75th Rangers, respectively. He was awarded several valor medals, including the Silver Star.

- Grif

THE RENDEZVOUS CONTINUES, VICTORY IS OUR HISTORY

Pete Griffin

Spring flowers, a new birth, greet Memorial Day,
The solemn day, we have chosen to pray......
To take the time, to give our thanks,
To salute warriors, no longer in our ranks.....

Wars have claimed, so many lives,
From their deaths, freedom thrives.....
Standing on these hallowed grounds,
We honor those, who made our nation sound.....

General William C. Lee stated in our birthing,
"The 101st Airborne Division has no history,
But it has a rendezvous with destiny.".....
"The RENDEZVOUS CONTINUES,
VICTORY IS OUR HISTORY"....

This magnificent monument stands to attest,
Our warriors sacrifices, courage and deaths...
We salute these loved ones, our country's best,
For love of country, they sleep in eternal rest....

The Screaming Eagle is poised to STRIKE,
Its powerful division, protects our rights.....
Our battle honors, carved below "Old Abe",
Warning freedom's enemies, they must behave...!

All around us, so many graves,
We owe to each, our thanks and praise...
For all of us, they paid the price,
For all of us, they gave their lives....

Memorial Day, a time to remind us,
The benefactors of our nation's finest.....
They have given us, security, peace and freedom,
Their bounty, the fruits of their seasons.....

Throughout our history, they answered the call,
They served their country, stood proud and tall.....
Their courage would not permit, our flag to fall,
For Duty, Honor, Country, they gave their all.........

Because of them, we are, "One Nation, Under God"
We live, work and play, on freedom's sod.....
Lady Liberty's torch of freedom, burns bright,
Their sacrifices have ensured our rights....

They lead the way, we too, must pay our dues,
Airborne Soldiers won't permit us to lose....
Freedom flourishes, in this land that we love,
In our skies, THE EAGLE PROTECTS THE DOVE....!

An unbroken line, freedom is nurtured
Soldiers of past, present and future...
Our freedom will never be lost,
Their efforts and sacrifices, never for naught.....

We keep in our hearts, what their deaths have taught,
We cherish our freedoms, the reasons they fought....
They set the example, "Freedom is not free".....
THE RENDEZVOUS CONTINUES,
VICTORY IS OUR HISTORY.

Photo: 101st Monument at Arlington Cemetery

HIS LOVE HAS NO END

Oh, so many blessings,
God has granted us,
But only love, oh so holy,
oh so timeless....

Love, so pure,
needs no refinement,
It has no bounds,
not even death,
can confine it....

Death can cast its sorrow,
darkness and gloom,
Love shines through,
to brighten and bloom....

Through trials and hardships,
love grows stronger,
Love, perpetual, eternity,
lasts no longer....

The keeping of peace,
the duty of the soldier,
The horrors of war,
carried on his shoulders....

He will lay down his life,
for his friend,
There is no greater love,
HIS LOVE HAS NO END....

PRAYER TO SAINT MICHAEL
(FOR PARATROOPERS)

Dear Saint Michael, protector of Heaven's Gate,
Guide your paratroopers, to a victorious fate...
Please keep us safe, in peace or war,
To right the wrongs, that God abhors....

Grant us speed, the flight of your wings,
The element of surprise, to deliver our sting....
Give our weapons, the fighting edge of your sword,
Equip us well, your AIRBORNE wards....

Protect our flesh, with your heavenly shield,
Your warrior heart, that we won't yield.....
Grant us strength, to endure the hardships,
Fairness in dealing, with those who would harm us....

Bend your wings, to form our perimeters,
That no enemy assault, could ever wither...
Grant us courage in attack,
Protect our flanks, and our backs....

Pray for us, on bended knee,
Lead us through hell, to victory....
To God's enemies, grant your vision to see,
That evil will fall, to those who are free....

Tell them, freedom is a gift from God,
"The Home of The Brave", his blessed sod....
"America, America, God sheds his grace on thee"
Saint Michael, patron saint of paratroopers,
lead us to victory!

Dedicated in loving memory and respect to Father Francis L. Sampson, our beloved "Paratrooper Padre" and protege of Saint Michael, Patron Saint of Paratroopers.

A MONUMENTAL TASK

```
You Screaming Eagles,
always so proud true,
In peace or war, protect
the red, white and blue....
Victory by plane, glider,
helicopter, since World War II,
Gallantly fulfill
your Airborne rendezvous....!
History records the heroic
deeds of your heritage,
Help salute YOUR Division
that you love and cherish....
"Old Abe", calls upon you, again,
to ask....?
Hook up, trooper,
for A MONUMENTAL TASK...!!!
```

LEST WE FORGET

Solemn memories, of Screaming Eagles, fallen,
Lost to battle, they answered the calling....
Of all they gave, the loves they lost,
Stolen years, but not for naught....

They left behind, so many blessings,
Throughout America, freedom is ringing....
Old Glory waves, from sea to shining sea,
God given rights, they secured, for you and me....

They paid the price for victory,
They have rendezvoused with destiny....
Now, we must preserve their legacy,
What will our future be?
LEST WE FORGET, OUR PROUD HISTORY...!!

LOOK out For
AIRBORNE'S PAPER TIGER

Gallant tales of the combat paratrooper,
are well known,
But in our shadow, there is a hero,
rarely shown....
Sharp and fast,
AIRBORNE'S PAPER TIGER,
has a mighty roar,
Wielding a weapon mightier than the sword ... !

His eyes and ears, always on full alert,
Quick and eager to spring to work....
Unnoticed, scurrying behind the scenes,
A staunch and faithful ally, rarely seen....

Nothing passes, that he doesn't see,
Ever vigilant to destroy our enemies....
Everything that crosses his path,
He takes accurate note and reports it fast....

Spreading the word far and wide,
Through vicious battles, he was by our side ....
For when he roared, the truth was heard,
Enemy propaganda was quickly discerned ...

A Master Parachutist,
awarded the Meritorious Service Medal,
the Bronze Star, The Combat Infantry Badge,
he has fought hard and traveled far....
Our Public Information Officer in Viet Nam,
Carrying pen and rifle he had no qualms... !

Serving in peace as well as war,
This dedicated soldier has kept our score....
After rounding out a distinguished AIRBORNE career,
By our side, he has stayed, throughout the years..

A pillar in his community, he has always been,
To The Boy Scouts of America, a true and loyal friend....
A professional fund raiser, there is no better,
An executive, publisher, editor, a real go getter...

A loving husband and father, faithful and true,
Four grandchildren, one great grandchild new...
An elder in his faith, setting an example,
for me and you,
Part Cherokee Indian, his GREAT SPIRIT
always comes through...

The 101st, the 82nd and Special Forces,
An AIRBORNE soldier whose mastered all courses....
He's afforded recognition and honor to all deserved,
In film and print, Airborne deeds he has preserved...

He has dedicated his professional life
to his beloved "Sky Soldiers",
Volumes of Airborne history,
borne on his shoulders....
Through his hard work,
determination and perseverance,
The Airborne has had a strong voice,
for all to hear us ... !

Retired Major Ivan Worrell
is of whom I speak,
His mighty roar blasts out
Airborne's courageous feats....
Impossible to spread our proud history
farther or wider,
No enemy could ever silence,
AIRBORNE'S PAPER TIGER...

INFINITY, SO CLOSE TO HOME

When I look into the nighttime sky,
I can't help, but wonder why . . . ?
Why . . . ? Can insignificant me,
See all the way, to infinity . . .?

The wonders of the great immense,
Oh so clear and evident ....
Everything, so precisely put,
Not one thing, underfoot....!

Everything in its proper place,
Order and sequence, suspended in space....
So many miles, between Heaven and Earth,
One can't imagine, its beginning, its birth....

Mankind, God's favorite creation,
Should be filled with, excitement, fascination...
No time to worry, hate or fight,
It's so clear, what's wrong, what's right...!

Our universe, so huge, so magnificent,
It's beauty, the ultimate entertainment....
There's so much to see and discover,
The greatness of God, is ours to wonder...

Millions of miles, just how high is the sky...?
Man's ultimate peak, can be seen in a smile...
Appreciating one another, so simple and easy,
We can attain this height, stomachs not queasy....

God made it, so easy to see,
Life on Earth can be heavenly...!
All that we, may want or need,
Can be ours, if we just take heed...

Obey God's word, praise his name,
Avoid what's wrong, the devil's game....
All of us can live in harmony,
Just pray to him, on bended knees...!

Be self content, the sky's the limit,
We all can be, God's highest summit....
Once there, we'll see, God's Heavenly throne,
Eternity will be, so pleasant to roam....
INFINITY, SO CLOSE TO HOME !!

THE MEEK WILL INHERIT THE EARTH

Thinking back, across the years,
Of times so hard, of times of fears....
The complex haze, begins to slowly, disappear,
Our loving God, making it crystal clear....

War has always, troubled our times,
It has taken its toll, on yours and mine....
But it has failed, to erase, the good in man,
For goodness was formed, by God's own hands....

He has planted it deep, within our souls,
Nothing pleases him more, than to see it grow
War - when evil walks, on God's good earth,
Tis the trial, to prove man's worth....

Satan places temptations, all along our way,
Those who partake, are sure to stray....
They will no longer follow, God's most holy path,
Their greed and hatred, will bring his wrath...!

When God and human dignity, can suffer no more,
Saint Michael's trumpet blares, the call to war....
Goodness must meet evil, on the fields of battle,
The sabers of righteousness, will be heard to rattle.. !

As the evils of war, claims the lives of the good,
It unknowingly strengthens, God's brotherhood....
It forms an army, it cannot defeat,
It gathers God's warriors, from the meek....

God's enemies, that have fallen,
Will set an example, to answer his calling...
The brothers of sin, punished by him,
Pay with their souls, the wages of sin...!

The loved ones we lost, God does herald,
This knowledge will comfort us, through our perils....
For these losses, are for all our good,
Their voices call out, for all of man,
to live as we should...!

For our swords, to remain as plowshares,
For all of mankind, we must sincerely care....
Only we, can stop having, to prove our worth,
If we obey God's laws,
THE MEEK WILL INHERIT THE EARTH...!

TO FOLLOW THAT STAR

A Christmas tradition, we need to start,
an expression of thanks, from the heart....
On our family Christmas tree, an ornamental soldier, place, for all to see...

A salute, to our soldiers, so far away, not home, to share, the holidays....
For the lonely GI, standing guard, protecting us, from all harm....

For our sailors, on great ships, a silent prayer, on our lips....
"God bless those, who sail the seas, preserving peace and democracy"....

For the Marines, who storm ashore, to raise the flag, we so adore....
For our Air Force, soaring through hostile skies,
risking all, so freedom thrives....

But most of all, to always remember, Fallen Heroes, of lost Decembers...
Of gallant deeds and supreme sacrifice,
TO FOLLOW THAT STAR, that shines so bright...

AMERICA'S WAR BIRD

SCREAMING EAGLES OF ALL TIMES,
ALWAYS ALERT, MAN THE FIRING LINES...
EVER VIGILANT, POISED TO STRIKE,
TO ENGAGE ALL ENEMIES, DAY OR NIGHT.....

GALLANT WARRIORS OF WORLD WAR II,
CHASED HITLER, CROSS THE RHINE, SO BLUE....
FROM NORMANDY TO BERCHTESGADEN,
SWASTIKAS FELL, FOREVER ROTTEN....

IN VIETNAM'S JUNGLES, OUR TROOPERS FOUGHT,
NEVER ONCE, A BATTLE LOST....
LIGHTNING TROOPERS OF IRAQ AND KUWAIT,
SADAM'S ARMIES, THEY LAID TO WASTE.....

ENEMIES OF THE FUTURE, BE AWARE!
"OLD ABE" WILL STRIKE, FROM THE AIR...
THE SCREAM OF THE EAGLE, WILL BE HEARD,
YOU BEST AVOID, AMERICA'S WAR BIRD....

PRESERVE THE SPIRIT

To jump from an aircraft, while in flight,
Into the blackness, of the night.....
The toughest mission, AIRBORNE, gets the nod,
Sky soldiers, beat the odds....

Unfamiliar terrain, inclement weather,
A determined enemy, all the better....!
Outnumbered and outgunned?
THE AIRBORNE SPIRIT, gets the job done....!

Hitting the ground, ready to fight,
Soon, your enemy, takes to flight.......
For they learn, they cannot defeat,
THE AIRBORNE SPIRIT, of the elite!

Strap your helmets, round your chin,
Check your equipment, stand in the door!
Another mission, you're called to win;
THE AIRBORNE SPIRIT must continue to soar!

If you must, pull your reserve,
THE AIRBORNE SPIRIT, we must preserve!
Send your contribution today,
It's the smallest price, we've had to pay!

AIRBORNE ALWAYS

Eagles fallen? Courageous troopers, how can this be?
For, from their deaths, bloomed victory....
Dedicated soldiers, to country and flag,
In pastures of green, their bodies were laid....

Are crosses of white, all that remain?
Headstones of granite, just bearing their names?
A brief ceremony, the playing of Taps,
The drying of tears, does their memory, just lapse?

Never, never, cry you and me,
For in their deaths, springs our destiny....
Forever, they will be, an integral part of "thee",
Always, always, our blessed family....

For all we are, for all we'll ever be,
We owe to them, "our country tis of thee"...
Our freedom of religion, our praying to God,
Because of them, He's blessed our sod....

For this, "the land of the free",
Without the brave, could never be....
Eagles fallen? A terrible loss.
For our future, they paid the cost...!

Eagles fallen? Nay, nay, this will never be,
For their spirit soars, through eternity....
Their bodies at rest, rightfully so,
But through their spirits, liberty flows....

This day of remembrance, we do share,
To let them know, forever we'll care...!
In our hearts and minds, their love we keep,
For only in history, do they rest in peace....

Eagles fallen? No, they have not,
For eagles soar, it is their lot....
Though they rest, on perch, so high,
Their spirit still protects, our lands and skies....

For we know, their spirit lives,
For AIRBORNE SPIRITS, continue to give....
By their example, we surely can rely,
For "THE SCREAMING EAGLE", can not die...!

America's freedoms will survive,
For young eagles, fill the skies...!
Never, never, no eagles fallen,
For their spirit, still answers the calling...!

THE SCARRED SHEPHERD

Invasive thoughts fill your mind,
Traumatic events, preserved in time....
Confusion is your state of mind,
Peace, so allusive, you'll never find. . .

Not permitted, don't shed a tear,
That tell-tale sign of confusion and fear....
At all costs, ignore the pain,
Or forever, endure the shame....

Flashbacks and night-mares come without warning,
The battle rages, enemy hordes are storming....
Oh, so vulnerable, there's little defense,
No place secure, in a jungle so dense....

The enemy lurks behind every bush,
You'll not see him, no use to look....
Camouflage, his devilish specialty,
Invisible, amongst the bamboo and trees....

Machine guns roar, soldiers bleed,
They cry for medics, in their need....
You try to reach them, for God's sake,
Awesome fire prevents, each attempt you make...

The enemy lets you hear them die,
Nothing you can do, to stop their cries...
Another attempt, you make,
Dodging bullets, as they rake....

Can not save them, no matter what you do,
Utter helplessness, for them and you....
A compassionate God, calls them home,
This haunting image, in your mind, will roam....

The dead and dying, everywhere,
Enemy voices, oh so near....
Gather your wits, show no fear,
Open fire, their flesh does tear....

"Fire, fire, kill them all,"
You must answer that battle call...
Hear them moan, see them fall,
They've put your back, against the wall....

Bodies decompose and begin to swell,
Rigor mortis gives off, such rancid smells....
Blood, wounds and flesh, so quick to decay,
Such horrific sights, in your mind, will stay....

When it's over, you're forever changed,
You won the battles, but bear the blame....
Protesters and politicians caused the war to be lost,
But only the warriors will bear the cost....

"Forget the war, get on with your life,
Ignorant words, that cut like a knife....
Hold your tongue, they don't understand,
THE SCARRED SHEPHERD, who protected the lambs....

WHERE THE EAGLE PROTECTS THE DOVE

God bless this land we love,
WHERE THE EAGLE PROTECTS THE DOVE
Where our children grow up free,
In Your land of opportunity....

From the cool, clear waters of Puget Sound,
To Florida's white sands, renown....
From the shores of our Great Lakes,
Across our deserts and plains so great....

God bless each and every state,
Bestow on us, Thy saving grace....
Save us from Satan's evil fate,
Liberty and justice, be our sacred mates....

God bless our people, of every race,
Let equality reflect, on every face....
Race, creed or color, be no disgrace,
Our hands clasped in sincere embrace....

Bring gentle rain, to moisten our soil,
The sweat of our labor, to flower from toil....
Send subtle winds, to caress our wheat,
Provide your people, blessed manna to eat....

Let the sun shine, to brighten our days,
"The beginning of wisdom, fear of Yahweh"....
"One nation, under God", we kneel and pray,
For truth and righteousness, to lead our way....

Let the "Stars and Stripes", wave and greet,
All earth's people, seeking peace....
Let our example, shine clear and bright,
So all the world's nations, see Your light.....

Where the strong protect the weak,
Where the brave respect the meek....
Where the rich, share with the poor,
America, be the world's
persecuted peoples' open door...!

From Alaska's snow capped peaks,
To Hawaii's orchids, so sweet....
God bless this land we love,
WHERE THE EAGLE PROTECTS THE DOVE.

YOU HAVE THE RIGHT

What is a liberal? Just what do they say?
They promote individual rights, do it their way...
Question authority, no matter the purpose,
Their self serving reasons, it's moral treason.... !

If it feels good, DO IT, create a fad,
Don't really matter, if the outcome is bad....
Religious beliefs are just a constraint,
Forget about God; immorality , not their complaint ....

Decadent behavior, a personal right,
Consenting adults, don't wait till the night.... .
Homosexuals, should be most proud,
Get a flag, have a parade, form a crowd....!

Freedom FROM religion, an absolute necessity,
Support atheists, agnostics, that's the remedy.......
Stop prayer in schools, it's unconstitutional,
'The Pledge of Allegiance', a brainwashing tool . . . !

Patriotic beliefs will get you killed,
Support your country Liberal Blood, not spilled....
Disruptive behavior, twisted values,
Gays in the military, lovers are conciliatory...!

Capital punishment, unusual and cruel,
Killers are good people, they merely broke a rule ...!
The police, courts, the whole penal system,
Are inept, they are without wisdom....

Freedom of speech, the Liberal's battle cry
Pornography is OK, unbare those thighs...!
No matter the audience, no matter their age
Stifling expressions, brings their outrage....

Women have rights, it's their body,
Unborn babies, an unwanted commodity...!
Abortion it's just a birth control,
Taxes should pay, its obscene toll...!

Entertainment should have no bounds,
Vulgarity, violence, pornography, have legal grounds...!
Liberals have the right to advertise as they please,
Polluting our homes with their television sleeze...!

ALL WARS are wrong, there's no reason to die,
No matter atrocities, abuses and lies....
It's over there, we must not interfere,
Our security, not threatened,
WE MUST STEER CLEAR...!

Human suffering is OK,
If it don't affect me in a personal way,
It's OK to rape, rob, and pillage,
The criminals are just so underprivileged,
No problem, just don't victimize me or my village....!

Cigarette smoking, a most terrible thing,
It pollutes the air, causes suffering....
Smokers shouldn't have rights, such a nasty habit,
Why don't they have sex, act like us rabbits....!!!!

Religious beliefs and family values,
Only restrict, they will assail you....
Don't let them tell you what to do,
Pierce your ears, get a tattoo, dye your hair blue....

Welfare is our fifty-first state,
Divorced, one parent family, most commonplace....
Go to Family Court, liberals offer vast support,
Just tax dollars, of no import...!

Join our ranks, there is no evil,
Paint what you want, on OUR EASEL....
We know how, NOT, to pay the bill,
Let the taxpayer do it, put us on Capitol Hill.....

Be gay, live life the ACCEPTABLE, alternative way,
Don't let this be! Innocent people suffer needlessly...!
Trauma victims receive contaminated blood,
EMT's MUST wear gloves...!

Extra precautions waste time and money,
Innocent people ARE DYING, honey...
The "Golden Hour" slides by fast,
When trauma centers MUST SLOW their tasks...!!!

You may watch YOUR CHILDREN die,
YOU TOO, should your sex partner lie...!!!!
Six out of ten hemophiliacs have HIV,
They didn't catch it, living "alternatively"...!!!!!!

Their goal in life, keep their name off "THE QUILT"!!!!!
They pay the price, but they're free of guilt...!!!
Ryan White, surely forced to pay,
Addicts or gays, sure shortened his days...!!!!!!!

Liberals, doesn't matter if they're wrong or right,
The more of them, the more their might,
All is OK, don't be afraid of the night,
Keep voting liberal, YOU HAVE THE RIGHT...!!!!!

FREEDOM IS NOT FREE

The horrors of war, unfleshed, you did not see,
You know naught, the price of victory ....
You only understand, "me, myself and I,"
Forgotten, unknown soldiers, the only ones to die ...

Free..! You abort your babies, take your drugs,
Play golf at your country clubs ....
Drink your cocktails, play sexual games,
Money, money, your power and fame ...

Top shelf, your only desire,
No manual labor, that's for hire ...
Catered to, from head to toe,
In your limousine, off you go ....

Rhodes scholars - slick politicians,
the best you could buy,
Thousand dollar words, disguise all lies ...
The cycle of poverty, you refuse to break,
Hard working people, won't fill your ranks ....

Now, everything is going your way,
The poor, without roots, so easy in sway ....
The White House, so elegantly maintained,
Well disguised, hiding your shame ....

All is swell, the economy, fine,
Only morality has decayed, in your climb ....
But watch your step, for certainly, you'll fall,
When you do, you're going to crawl ....

For God, now your enemy, is at your gates,
Terror will open your eyes, but it's too late .....
Retribution, by God , be your fate,
For arrogance and decadence, you did mate ....

Thousand dollar words, will no longer sway,
For, justice, now rules the day ....
The whole earth, He will not flood,
But you'll drown, in your bitter blood ....

First person singular, you do understand,
America, no longer, seems your land ....
But in its new society, you will fit,
Serving the poor, just- for tips ... !!!!

TOMORROW is now today,
The liberal machine has had its way ....
An idol fills our dishonoured throne,
The brave no longer, feel at home ....

For years, combat veterans, put in their place,
Betrayed and cast into cocooned disgrace ....
Their voices, stifled, by the vocal majority,
Their sacrifices labeled, misguided disloyalty ....

For decades, you liberals, free, to do as you pleased,
Perfunctory worship, won't soil your knees ....
Insatiable pleasure seekers, that you are,
Your appetites reach beyond the stars ....

This poem, I know, you'll refuse to hear it,
You're not one, to grin and bear it ....
But said, it will be done,
Because freedoms, by patriot's blood, have been won....

Unlimited money can not buy them,
But certainly, "FREEDOM IS NOT FREE"....
How then, did you obtain them...?
Simply, inherited, to your glee ...

Possession, just part of your properties,
Forgetting, "DUTY, HONOR, COUNTRY,"
PAID THE FEES ....
You think tax dollars, paid your dues,
But their real cost, you don't have a clue ...

GROWING COLD ... ?

Waiting for battle, you empty your bladder,
Control of your nerves, you must gather ....
You and your buddies, grow impatient,
All pray to God, for salvation ....

You think of home, your loved ones there,
What you could lose, heightens your fears ....
Fight you will, must hold your own,
Can not dwell on the pleasures of home ....

Hyper-vigilant, you must be,
Stay alert, so tomorrow, you'll see ....
For everyday, you stay alive,
Betters the chances, you'll survive ....

Adrenaline flowing, the battle thrilling,
You fight hard, add to the killing ....
For kill you must, you have no choice,
You hear a scream, it be your voice ....

You see them die, be friend or foe,
Can't permit, your emotions show ....
A sign of weakness, you can't display,
Your innermost thoughts, you can't relay ....

To see the casualties, by the score,
Embeds in your mind, the horrors of war ....
You must do your duty, you are a soldier,
Fight you do, can't give no quarter ....

They keep coming, can't believe the carnage,
Hold your ground, fear you must harness ....
Snake and nape, fill the air,
Heat from explosions, your flesh does sear ....

More determined, with each attack,
How much longer, can this last ... ?
Hear the bullets, striking flesh,
The smells of war, fill each breath ....

As you look, you see friends fall,
Must counterattack, and kill them all ....
"Charge, charge, take that hill,"
The spirit of the bayonet, "kill, kill, kill"....

Suddenly, the battle ends,
A gentle rain, God does send ....
As if He wants, to wash away,
The death that happened, on this day ....

As you scan the battlefield,
The blood and gore makes you reel ....
Bodies lying all over the place,
A look of "Why?", froze on their face ....

The smells make your stomach retch,
Insects feeding, as you gasp for breath ....
The wounded groaning, crying for help,
Gather your wits, control yourself ....

To the wounded, you do give aid,
Never knowing, if life, you saved ....
Victory, the battlefield, you do possess,
Room, to bury the dead, in due process ... ?

The sound of helicopters, fill the air,
Pop green smoke, there's no enemy snare ....
Medevacs load the wounded,
Their thump, thump, thump, so very soothing....

Slicks and gunships also land,
Here to offer, a helping hand ... ?
Oh so glad, the battle over,
Relieved to be, one day older ....

As I watch, myself, I question,
What will I learn, from this lesson ... ?
Will I be changed, forever after,
In my life, still room for laughter ... ?

A gallant action, they say, "We won"....
Got the enemy, on the run ....
"Saddle up, lock and load"
Is only their trail, GROWING COLD...?

Letter Home

Dear Mom, Dad and folks,

Just a few minutes to drop you a line. Have a funny feeling I'm running out of time. Set up a defense around the artillery, last night. Charlie decided it was a good time to fight. Sent a battalion in the middle of the night. "A" Company put up a hell of a fight. They had us outnumbered four to one, thought they had us, when it begun. Got our act together quick as we could, seems Charlie only fights in his own neighborhood. Came out of the jungle, bugles and whistles blowing. Heavy machineguns and AK tracers glowing. Hollering at us, "Tonight you die!", had us believing, it wasn't a lie.

They were trying hard to knock out our heavy guns, but the artillery only lost but one. It changed hands a couple of times, when the enemy broke through our lines. They tried their best to overrun our positions, but these troopers upheld the "Screaming Eagle" tradition. One new trooper said, with tears in his eyes, "They got us surrounded, the poor bastards", but our flag was still on it's standard. He thought it was time for "Taps". I was scared too, but couldn't help but laugh.

Some of the NVA had ropes tied to their ankles, about fifteen feet long. When they die, their buddies pull them back where they belong. They don't want us to know how many we've killed. Hinders the count, but no denying, bloods been spilled. They hide the bodies in the jungle, don't know why they go to the trouble. After a few days they don't smell like a rose, all we have to do is follow our nose.

At the peak of the fight, didn't seem we'd make it through the night. They were hitting us from all four sides. The guys on our listening posts were caught outside, they had to run for their lives. Charlie was right on their butts, most made it back, but it was luck. When Charlie got on line and made his push, seemed like there was one behind every bush. All the sudden they would charge, our howitzers fired point blank, a most deadly barrage. Beehive rounds found their marks, the dead were everywhere. The "Redlegs" instilled in them a most terrible fear. It was amazing, the punishment they took. If they had stopped, just long enough to look, there wasn't enough rope to tie each foot. Nor arms enough to pull them back, they lost that many in the attack.

Our engineers had to pick up their rifles and join the fight. Many of them became heroes last night. They fought like hell, their M 16's blazing, the effect of their grenades, amazing. They left many enemy soldiers dead and lame. Great soldiers, these Combat Engineers, they have earned their name. They should be listed in the annals of Infantry fame.

Our commanders called in air strikes, they pounded the enemy throughout the night. "Smokey the Bear" dropped flares, created an eerie light. But it was good enough to see, the ravaged enemy retreat in disharmony. "Puff the Magic Dragon" came in for the kill, laying hot lead all over those hills.

Most of the guys think the battles done, but I have a nagging feeling, Charlie isn't really on the run. Still have that feeling, I'm running out of time. Oh well, don't worry, I'll be fine. Will write again, they are probably right, ain't many Charlies, survived last night. Remember all, I love you much, think of me, wish me luck.

Your Soldier.

(IN MEMORY OF OUR FALLEN SOLDIERS OF OPERATION HAWTHORNE)

By: Peter S. Griffin
    Co. A, 2/502nd Infantry
    101st Airborne Division
    Viet Nam, 1965-66

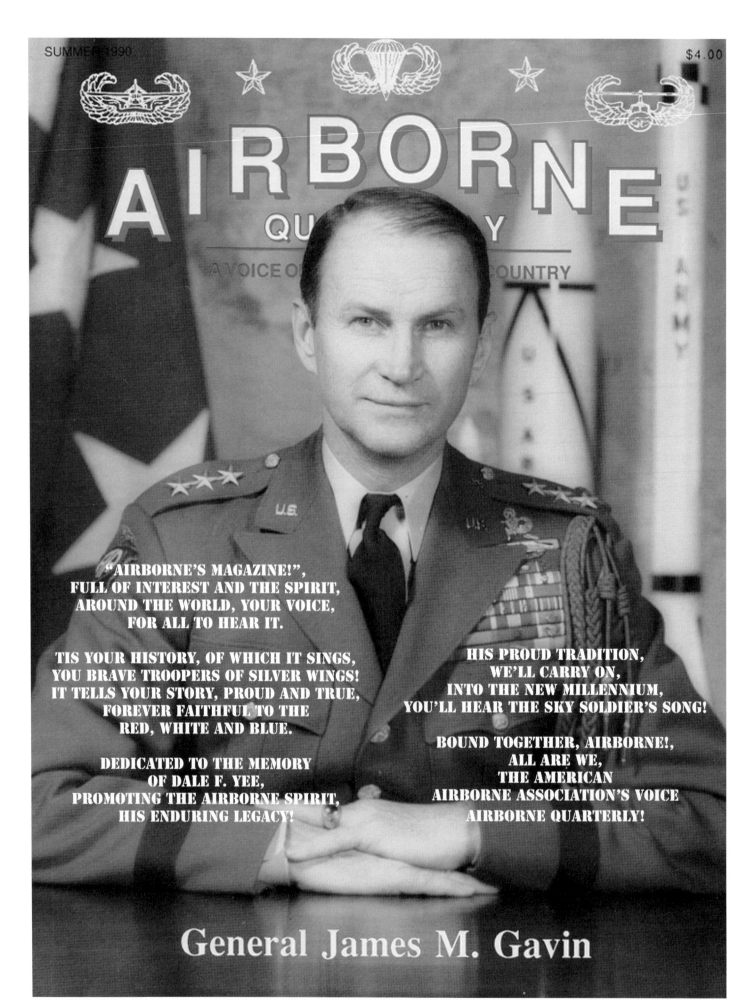

SUMMER 1990 $4.00

AIRBORNE
QUARTERLY
A VOICE OF THE COUNTRY

"AIRBORNE'S MAGAZINE!",
FULL OF INTEREST AND THE SPIRIT,
AROUND THE WORLD, YOUR VOICE,
FOR ALL TO HEAR IT.

TIS YOUR HISTORY, OF WHICH IT SINGS,
YOU BRAVE TROOPERS OF SILVER WINGS!
IT TELLS YOUR STORY, PROUD AND TRUE,
FOREVER FAITHFUL TO THE
RED, WHITE AND BLUE.

DEDICATED TO THE MEMORY
OF DALE F. YEE,
PROMOTING THE AIRBORNE SPIRIT,
HIS ENDURING LEGACY!

HIS PROUD TRADITION,
WE'LL CARRY ON,
INTO THE NEW MILLENNIUM,
YOU'LL HEAR THE SKY SOLDIER'S SONG!

BOUND TOGETHER, AIRBORNE!,
ALL ARE WE,
THE AMERICAN
AIRBORNE ASSOCIATION'S VOICE
AIRBORNE QUARTERLY!

General James M. Gavin

IMAGES...

The rainbows' colors;
Joined one by one...
Life's storm be done.

War destroys life,
Be it acceptable...
If not yours..?

Life leaves the body;
Without a trace...
In need of grace?

Observing death;
A tragic thing...
The loss of being.

Traumatic loss;
Quick as a wink...
Lifetime to think!

Forever young;
When you are so...
Old, before you know.

Love is infinite;
Life so short...
Ours to abort..?

Hug your child;
For awhile...
Before life expires!

Slow down;
Life goes by fast..
Make it last!

Take a breath;
Fill your lungs...
Contentment done.

Pollution in mind;
Can't be kind...
Love so fine.

God is love;
Just look about...
Be little doubt!

The heavens aloft;
Just look above...
The peace of doves.

God's open arms;
Grant us life...
But only twice.

Walk on earth;
Ye noble man...
Only one clan.

Procreation's tool;
Sex...
Abused by fools!

God Almighty;
Forgive us...
Rightly..?

In little minds-,
Hate grows fast...
But, can forever last.

Respect one and all;
Mankind stands tall...
Satan will fall !

Peace on earth;
Ultimate worth...
From God's birth!

Shake one's hand;
Tis God's plan...
In the promised land!

From sea to sea;
On briny foam...
Peace brings sailors home.

Music; God pleasing;
Meant to be...
Heavenly.

Sitting at home alone;
Life wastes away...
Friendship paves the way.

A sincere prayer;
God listens...
Tarnish glistens.

A true friend;
Never dies...
Enhances lives.

Righteousness thrives;
In hearts wise...
Hatred dies.

God sheds light;
For blindness to see...
His Holy Trinity.

Freedom's continuity;
Does depend...
Will you defend..?

How can it be;
God's image and likeness...
Climbed down from trees..?

Family preservation;
God's elation...
Make notation.

Soldiers, sailors, marines,
Coast guard, airmen...
Let's just thank them.

Just discipline,
Our children need...
Permissiveness they do plead.

Trust in God;
All be right...
End bloody strife.

Stars and stripes;
Red, white and blue...
America be me and you!

_____

My Wife

Thank you for being MY WIFE,
Thank you for sharing my life....
Many years have come and gone,
Both our children, proud and grown....

From state to state, from house to home,
With you by my side, I was never alone...
Standing by me, through thick and thin,
No better a wife, no better a friend....

When times were bad, and I was quite sad,
Sick or hurt, making it worse....
I always had you, to see me through,
Better days, were never far away....

Your constant smile, your attentive ear,
Kept me from falling, into despair....
Your loving embrace, saw me through,
Thank you for being so true....

I always tried, but sometimes failed,
To do my best, making right prevail....
Beaten down, not knowing why,
I always got up, with you by my side....

To fight PTSD, to carry on,
You helped me up, you made me belong....
Now we have a much better life,
Only because, I have you for MY WIFE....

I want you to know, that I love you so,
Thank you for helping me grow....
Thank you for helping me see,
But most of all, thank you, for believing in me....

Perhaps now, while we have the chance,
Our life will be happy, full and balanced....
I thank God for all you do,
For blessing me, with a wife like you....

For blessing us in so many ways,
For giving us grandchildren, to watch at play....
For all this, I'll thank Him, the rest of my days,
For the love of MY WIFE, God's shining rays....

For the love of my life, For MY WIFE, Brenda Gibson

Intercession Letter to Saint Michael

(For Veterans)

Dear Saint Michael,
the Archangel,

I continue to beseech you to protect me, my family and loved ones.
Please keep us safe from all harm and danger. Please protect us in our travels, works, homes, schools, and during our leisure hours. Please protect our property and our animals.
Please, also, keep us free from disease, drugs and alcohol. But, most of all, please help us in our fight against sin. I thank you, I honor you and I love you. Please pray for me, Saint Michael. Amen

THE GALLANT CORPS

The year two thousand will soon be here,
For Airborne history, a milestone year ....
A new millennium about to begin,
Airborne's sixtieth birthday, we'll ring in ....

What a history there is to relate,
Victory, after victory, we'll celebrate ....
Vertical assault warfare, passed many a test,
Sky warriors, proven, the best ....

When our elements attack from on high,
Enemy armies tremble, wither and die ....
This they know, when Airborne appears,
Cometh death, preceded by shock and fear...!

Airborne troop carriers flew through hostile skies,
Brave crews, stared death - straight in the eye ....
Paratroopers and Glidermen saved many a day,
Thanking the Pathfinders, who lit the way ....

Marine Recon, Beach Jumpers, Navy Seals - once UDT,
Brought many an enemy, to their knees ....
Special Forces wear the Green Beret,
Elite Rangers lead the way, their steel bayonets ending many a fray ...

Air Assault Troopers of helicopter attack,
Fast as lightning, they cut no slack ....
Air Force and Coast Guard have their elite,
Specialized missions, they bravely complete ....

Such awesome power, amassed and unleashed,
Condemns our enemies, to certain defeat ....
For earthly defenses can not withstand,
An Airborne envelopment battle plan ...!

So you warriors of silver wings,
Whatever your method, of you, history sings ....
For sixty years, you've stood in the door,
Preserving freedom, ALL AIRBORNE, THE GALLANT CORPS ...!

THE UNITED STATES OF AMERICA

TO ALL WHO SHALL SEE THESE PRESENTS, GREETING:

THIS IS TO CERTIFY THAT
THE PRESIDENT OF THE UNITED STATES OF AMERICA
AUTHORIZED BY ORDER OF
GENERAL GEORGE WASHINGTON, AUGUST 7, 1782
HAS AWARDED
(posthumously)

THE PURPLE HEART

TO

Corporal John T. Griffin, RA 12 297 322, Infantry

FOR

WOUNDS RECEIVED IN ACTION

resulting in his death 25 March 1951

GIVEN UNDER MY HAND IN THE CITY OF WASHINGTON
THIS 14th DAY OF May 1951

IN GRATEFUL MEMORY OF

Corporal John T. Griffin

WHO DIED IN THE SERVICE OF HIS COUNTRY

in the military operations in Korea
on March 25, 1951

HE STANDS IN THE UNBROKEN LINE OF PATRIOTS WHO HAVE DARED TO DIE

THAT FREEDOM MIGHT LIVE, AND GROW, AND INCREASE ITS BLESSINGS.

FREEDOM LIVES, AND THROUGH IT, HE LIVES—

IN A WAY THAT HUMBLES THE UNDERTAKINGS OF MOST MEN

Harry Truman

PRESIDENT OF THE UNITED STATES OF AMERICA

Shown are John Griffin's Purple Heart certificate and official report of his ultimate sacrifice for the cause of freedom. The Purple Heart Medal shown (back and front) belongs to Dale F. Yee.

Above: William J. Griffin, Jr. Company A,
1/188th Infantry, 11th Airborne Division
(1951).
Top: The RAKASSAN Memorial (187th ARCT)
at Fort Campbell, Kentucky.
Left: John T. Griffin, U.S. Navy (WWII).

Photo above, from left to right:
Mike Levart, "Buckey" and "DOC".

Mike Levart, a good friend of Pete Griffin, was shot three times
at Dak To during the summer of 1967.   He was a member of the
173rd Airborne Brigade.

Photo left: Pete Griffin in Vietnam (1965).

Below:
Three Sailors at Time Square
(left to right) Tom Cook,
Arnold, and John Griffin.

The Philippine Peso marking the
Allied Victory of World War II

Bottom:
Two Sailors
(left) Louie Eusepi with
        John Griffin.

SOUVENIR FROM TIMES SQ. NEW YORK

Third Class
Petty Officer
John T. Griffin,
U.S.N. - WWII

Lynn Griffin's engagement portrait - "My Sister, Dear..."

Above:
Pete Griffin
visits the Wall.

Right:
The Vietnam War
Memorial statue
of three G.I.'s.

Far right:
Peter Griffin's
Silver Star Award
certificate for
his distinguished
action during the
Dak To operations
(1966).

THE UNITED STATES OF AMERICA

TO ALL WHO SHALL SEE THESE PRESENTS, GREETING:

THIS IS TO CERTIFY THAT
THE PRESIDENT OF THE UNITED STATES OF AMERICA
AUTHORIZED BY ACT OF CONGRESS JULY 9, 1918
HAS AWARDED

THE SILVER STAR

TO
PETER S. GRIFFIN
(THEN PRIVATE FIRST CLASS, UNITED STATES ARMY)

FOR
GALLANTRY IN ACTION
IN VIETNAM FROM 7 JUNE 1966 TO 11 JUNE 1966
GIVEN UNDER MY HAND IN THE CITY OF WASHINGTON
THIS   2D   DAY OF   NOVEMBER   1995

THE ADJUTANT GENERAL

SECRETARY OF THE ARMY

The President of the United States of America, authorized by Act of Congress, July 9, 1918, has awarded the Silver Star to

PETER S. GRIFFIN
(THEN PRIVATE FIRST CLASS, UNITED STATES ARMY)

for gallantry in action:

Private First Class Griffin distinguished himself by gallantry in action from 7 June to 11 June 1966, while serving as a fire team leader with Company A, 2d Battalion (Airborne), 502d Infantry, 1st Brigade, 101st Airborne Division. During this period Private First Class Griffin's unit was engaged in continuous military operations involving conflict with an armed enemy force near Dak To, Republic of Vietnam. The acts of extraordinary heroism repeatedly displayed by Private First Class Griffin while engaging a numerically superior enemy force in close combat with both rifle fire and hand grenades contributed immeasurably to the prevention of the unit positions being overrun and the defeat of the enemy forces. Particularly noteworthy were his actions on the final night of conflict when unit members were hit after being ambushed by the enemy forces and he carried a severely wounded comrade throughout the night until contact was made with friendly forces. Private First Class Griffin's actions were in keeping with the highest traditions of the military service and reflects great credit upon him, his unit, and the United States Army.

Above:
Mrs.
Leita E.
Griffin,
Peter
Griffin's
mother.

Officer Griffin,
Oswego Police
Department, Oswego,
New York
(1968-1978).

Top/right:
Lynn (Griffin) and her husband, George.

Above: Pete and Brenda Griffin at the
1st Brigade Reunion, 101st - Fort

> Overleaf:
Co. A 2/502,
101st Airborne (1965).
Peter Griffin is second
row on right.

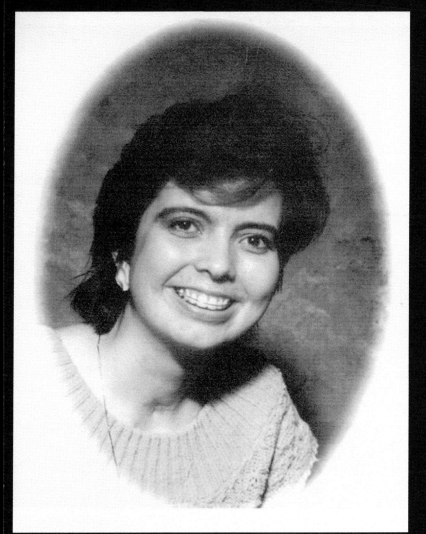

Above:
Grif visits West
Point, December
1995, when it was
freezing.

Top/left:
Pamela Griffin Law
(1986) taken after
recovery from a
terrible auto
accident
(see "Our Child Torn
and Tattered."
p. 117).

Korean War Memorial,
Washington, D.C.
(photo by Brenda Griffin).

MEMORIES

"Indecision is our worst enemy and our opponent's strongest ally!"

— Peter S. Griffin

THE WALL.....
A VETERAN'S VISIT

Names inscribed upon the wall,
Brings back memories of them all...
Fallen heroes who were slain,
Their sacrifice, honored, beautifully plain....

Name after name, I see the flames,
Vast sea of black, I see the flak....
Row after row, the battle grows,
Ammo they need, the more they bleed...

Viet Nam, so far away,
All the soldiers in harm's way....
Thinking back, another day,
Jungle thick, so many sick,
How can it be, they're calling me....

Reflections of a bygone era,
Clear as a bell, as if a mirror....
Whistles blow, the enemy close,
It is night, one hell of a fight,
When it's done, we have won....

But what a cost, so many lost,
My friends, you see, all brothers to me....
I look around, the crowd has grown,
The names I see, so many I've known,
Heroes all, they held their own....

A young girl, she asks of me,
Why oh why, how can this be?
They gave their lives, that's plain to see,
They gave it for you, they gave it for me,
They gave it so all- all, could be free....

It's quiet now, but people weep,
A silent prayer, for soldiers who sleep....
God bless you all, who answered the call,
You silent heroes of THE WALL.....

Sleep in peace, the battle's done,
Be it known, that you have won....
In the Kingdom of God, your life, will never end,
For, it was you, who laid down his life, for his friends...

The sentiments expressed in this poem arose during a Memorial Day visit by the author and his dear friend and former squad leader, Sergeant First Class (ret) James G. Moffitt....A brother true.

THE RISING SUN

Out of the East, the horror would come,
The dreaded war beast of **The Rising Sun**....
Sunday, December 7th of '41,
That day of infamy, the war had begun.....
  The Pacific Ocean was their nest,
  Full of warships, carriers the best...
  Tora, Tora, Tora!, was their call,
  A sneak attack would signal our fall....
Torpedo bombers led the way,
Pearl Harbor was sleeping, resting that day.....
Hickham Field was quiet, as well,
Soldiers at ease, Tojo quite pleased.....
  Devastation was thorough and quick,
  Japanese treachery had done the trick.....
  Our Pacific fleet was left in ruins,
  Sunken ships in a burning lagoon.....
Midway, Wake, and Guam fell next,
America's forces were most perplexed....
General MacArthur left the Philippines,
Japanese forces fulfilling their dreams.....
  British possessions in the Far East,
  Were soon to suffer, similar defeat.....
  Soldiers of **The Rising Sun**,
  Had the Allies on the run.....
Instilling terror everywhere,
Samurai Soldiers had nothing to fear.....
Gobbling up islands as they progressed,
Japs reveling in, such easy conquests....
  It wasn't long before we rallied,
  Our Air Forces would better the tally.....
  Doolittle and his Bombers filled the air,
  Soon Tokyo, would taste the fear....
Japanese Soldiers would fight to the death,
Suicide acceptable, if aided conquest.....
The "Bushido Code" called for this,
American power would grant them their wish.....
  Naval battles would turn the tide,
  Coral Sea, Midway, many Japs were to die....
  American Soldiers and Marines,
  Were soon to silence, the Banzai screams....

Our Merchant Marines joined the foray,
"The Red Ball Express" saved many a day.....
The Japanese were a bitter foe,
Jungle fighting was toe to toe....
  Heavy fighting was the theme,
  Island hopping was the scheme..
  Coast watchers monitored our foe,
  We'd attack as we'd grow....
Victories on Iwo Jima and Saipan,
Forced the Japs to alter their plans....
American flags, being raised everywhere,
Japanese losses, exploding in air.....
  MacArthur and Halsey gathered their might,
  Taking Leyte in the dark of night.....
  "Kamikazes" struck from the air,
  Jap desperation, reached a new tier.....
MacArthur's promise was right on,
American troops stormed Luzon....
Paratroopers jumped on Corregidor,
Airborne soldiers opened the door....
  "The Bataan Death March," horrors begotten,
  Japan's atrocities not forgotten......
  The Los Baños Raid, liberation at dawn,
  Paratroops jumped, to right such a wrong......
B29's bombed the Isles of Japan,
Fire bomb raids were scorching their lands.....
Jap industries burst into fire,
"Tokyo Rose" became known as a liar......
  To invade the land of **The Rising Sun**,
  America would lose, too many sons...
  On an August day, flew the "Enola Gay",
  Atomic blasts would finish the task....
Anchored in Tokyo Bay,
"Missouri Guns" seemed to sway.....
Leaders of **The Rising Sun**,
Had to answer, for what they done...
  September 2nd, of '45,
  "VJ Day" had finally arrived.....
  The Rising Sun was set by the best,
  "The Sleeping Giant" put them to rest....

D-DAY, A SOUND BEGINNING

Anticipation is a strange thing,
The invasion of Europe, in the offing...
Will we go, will we not,
My head is spinning, stomach in knots....

Boarding the plane, adjusting your gear,
None of the men, showing much fear....
Well briefed, we know what to expect,
Engines roaring, time to reflect....

Remembering home, the loved ones there,
Pleasant memories, planes take to the air....
Paratroopers will lead the way,
The invasion of France, is underway....

To catch the Germans by surprise,
Airborne soldiers, will jump and die....
"D-Day" has begun,
Soon, Hitler's armies on the run.....

Flying in the dark of night,
The planes are bobbing left and right,
Enemy guns are firing high,
Tracer bullets light up the sky....

June 6th, of forty-four,
Never have so many, stood in the door....
As the light turned from red to green,
"Bill Lee" was the scream....

Before I knew it, my chute was open,
Planes on fire, my breathe was choking....
Bullets flying, brave men dying,
Looking down, still hear the sounds....

German soldiers, running around,
Buildings on fire, throughout the towns....
Paratroopers landing everywhere,
Firing their "Thompsons" from the air....

The Cherbourg peninsula, all a drop zone,
Troopers and gliders, some landing alone.....
Clicking their "crickets" all did regroup,
Creating chaos, confusing Nazi troops....

Inflicting damage, wherever they went,
Enemy soldiers forced to relent....
Paratroopers were paving the way,
Seizing objectives and securing causeways.

To open exits for the beaches,
Seaborne troops would soon be reaching...
Normandy would soon be stormed,
Nazi soldiers not forewarned....

Caught unaware and by surprise,
Enemy soldiers were quick to die.....
Trying hard to hold their own,
Dying Nazi's were heard to groan.....

Heavy fighting, brought to bear,
Airborne victories were quite clear...
Germans couldn't counterattack,
Paratroopers would cut no slack.....

Capturing roadways, bridges and locks,
Airborne soldiers could not be stopped....
Taking objectives as they went,
Nazi resistance was badly spent.....

As a result of the Airborne mission,
Normandy's beaches became acquisitions...
H-Hour was a success,
Many Nazis' were laid to rest....

"D-Day" opened the door,
Allied victories thus assured....
Cherbourg became an open port,
Nazi Germany became a fort......

"D-Day, A Sound Beginning",
The sound of freedom, allies winning...
Twas the start of something great,
Airborne soldiers, sealing Hitler's fate....

The cost was high, the price was paid,
Many crosses mark their graves.....
Paratroopers fought and died,
But Europe's freedom still survives....
Thank you all, for what you've done,
You Airborne heroes, everyone...

Thanks to Russell A. Schwenk, F 2/506, for a great story - Grif / "Bill Lee" the Father of the Airborne.

DUTCH TREAT

"Dutch treat", everyone pays their way,
That's the way it was, that September day ....
Allied Airborne, honed and sharpened,
Paratroopers jumped on "Marketgarden"....

C47's filled the skies,
Nazi soldiers wouldn't believe their eyes....
A surprise attack, from the air,
Yanks, British, Poles, gliders everywhere...

Paratroopers jumped in broad daylight,
Never was seen, such an Airborne might. . .
To seize and hold, was their mission,
"Hell's Highway", no matter its condition....

To take the road, that was the key,
To unlock the doors of Germany ....
British armor would have to race,
Hope like hell they can stand the pace....

Paratroopers, proud and true,
Lightly armed, they'd see it through.....
Heavy guns must take up the slack,
To keep the Germans off their backs ....

The Dutch Underground was our eyes,
The Nazis' couldn't take us by surprise.....
With them fighting by our side,
The Germans could not turn the tide ....

Liberating towns as they went,
Airborne lives were being spent ....
Fighting hard, they made their way,
German soldiers were made to pay....

Eindhoven, Zon, St. Oedenrode,
Never have troopers been so bold.....
The Dutch people, filled with glee,
Ever so happy, for their liberty.....

Freeing all as they went,
the Airborne mission would not relent.....
Taking bridges as they progressed,
Defeating Germans in the process......

Vechel, Uden, Grave, and Nijmegan,
Freeing these towns, all in the bargain...
The 101st and 82nd were succeeding,
The German Army was sent reeling....

The British 1st Airborne was at Arnhem,
But Nazi Panzers were there to harm them...
Trying to take the bridge across the Rhine,
The British were running out of time.....

Forty eight hours were the most,
These British troopers could stay afloat...
Thirty Corps was still by the Waal,
If they didn't hurry, they would fall....

Situation desperate, some made their escape,
Trying to take Arnhem was a mistake ....
Had they reached the Zuider Zee,
"Marketgarden" would have been such a victory....

Airborne strength, by its self,
Accomplished more than was asked for......
But Arnhem was a "Bridge Too Far",
"Operation Marketgarden" was thus marred..

Ask the Dutch, just what they think,
"Marketgarden" had no kinks......
It freed their people and country,
They love the "Airborne" and their liberty.......

A highway divided was the mission,
An occupied country was the condition....
Freeing The Netherlands was a great feat,
To see them smile, is a "Dutch Treat"....

A TIME TO REMEMBER

Let us pause and reflect,
On a battle we'll never forget....
T'was December of '44,
All our troopers were at war....

Tested on OVERLORD and MARKETGARDEN,
Screaming Eagles, toned and hardened....
Fought their way to the Ardennes,
Never pausing to take a rest....

Knocking hard on Hitler's gate,
Paratroopers would seal his fate...
T'was their job to protect,
Bastogne's borders from conquest...

German armies had amassed,
This breakthrough would be the last....
To reach the Meuse, to tighten the noose,
To strangle the allies on the loose....

Artillery pounded day and night,
All of Belgium shook with fright....
T'was a mistake, the Germans thought,
Defending Bastogne, all would be lost....

"Send the message", their general said,
"Surrender now or you'll be dead...."
The 101st don't have a chance,
All will die by the Nazi lance....

Fighting sleep and bitter cold,
The 101st would surely fold....
Low on supplies and ammunition,
They'd surrender without condition....

The only thing he didn't consider,
Screaming Eagles would not wither....
Airborne soldiers tried and tested,
Their fighting spirit would not be bested...

General McAuliffe said one word,
They wouldn't believe what they heard....
What is this? "Nuts!" he said,
The Germans answered with armor and lead....

Artillery and armor, shells were cracking,
Nazi infantry were attacking....
Airborne courage was not lacking,
They'd fight like hell and wait for backing....

Holding on to precious ground,
Inflicting damage with every round....
Airborne soldiers fought and bled,
Winter's snow was turning red....

"The Battered Bastards Of Bastogne"
Fought like Belgium was their own...
Hold on they did, to turn the tide,
To attack when Patton arrived....

Allied armor to lend a hand,
They chased the Nazis to Rhineland....
Fighting hard as they went,
Their airborne spirit would not relent....

Over fifty years have come and gone,
Time can't diminish what they have done....
"The Battle Of The Bulge", was a hard fought one,
Belgium was free and the war was won....

These paratroopers of World War II,
Fought like hell and saw it through....
Screaming Eagles who fought and bled,
Their fighting spirit will never be dead....

Let us pause and reflect,
To give them honor and respect....
Our fallen brothers we'll never forget,
Their sacrifices are part of us yet...

Many crosses stand as a reminder,
Airborne soldiers have never been finer....
Screaming Eagles proud and true,
Defending freedom for me and you....

God bless them all, for what they've done,
Airborne heroes, everyone....
Hitler is finished, the world is free,
Let us celebrate the victory...!

VE DAY

VE day, what a wonderful thing!
Victory in Europe, just what does it mean?
To put into words, a challenging task,
So many battles, flags at half mast...

People have suffered, countries have fallen,
Soldiers that bled, heroes that led ....
Men into battle, prisoners like cattle,
Death camps in place, war's ugly face.....

Screeching rockets, sirens sounding,
Air raid coming, artillery pounding ....
Loved ones lost, what a terrible cost,
Children cry, their innocence lost ....

The Nazi Army on the march,
Punishment cruel, life is so harsh...
Enslaving people, burning steeples,
Cities in ruins, disease follows soon....

Blackouts at night, such terrible fright,
The earth is quaking, buildings shaking....
Nightmares most common, death so alarming,
Blood in the streets, bodies in heaps....

Spirits are low, no place to go,
Hitler is reigning, freedom is waning...
Hell is on earth, swastikas on perch,
Europe in trouble, must look to each other....

Human dignity will recover,
Freedom's torch will not be smothered...
Allied Armies are regrouping,
All our losses, we'll be recouping....

In our hearts we truly know,
Allied resolve will surely grow...
Enemy victories, to no avail,
Hitler's terror, will surely fail....

Britain is the staging point,
Men and equipment, all our might...
Highly trained and spirits soaring,
They will depart from England's moorings....

Allied aircraft darken the sky,
Dakotas and gliders flying high....
Full of paratroopers, ready to fight,
They will jump in the dark of night .....

Mighty warships crossing the Channel,
Full of soldiers, ready for battle....
They will attack from the sea,
Storming the beaches at Normandy....

Many battles follow D-Day,
Too many to mention, in a meaningful way....
Precious ground, paid for in blood,
Allied crosses erected in the mud...

Sweat, blood, and determination,
Freeing each and every nation....
Step by step, as they proceed,
Freeing all who are in need....

Starving people, a terrible sight,
Women and children, crying out in their plight....
Hitler's armies abusing their might,
They will fall, in a fair fight!

Battle after battle, the Axis fails,
Licking their wounds, to no avail....
St. Lo, Anzio, Bastogne and the Bulge,
Hitler will wish, he never was....

Losing battles all over the place,
Hitler afraid to show his face.....
Retreating to the Eagle's Nest,
He and Eva were laid to rest....

Heroes lost in battle, was the cost,
Lives gone, but not all lost....
God has given them eternal fame,
For their loss was our gain....

No greater gift could they give,
Than their love of brotherhood.....
Ghostly bugles sound their song,
"They Gave Their Lives To Right All Wrongs"....

So we should, as we go,
Live our lives in their shadows......
Good examples, all are they,
They still lead and show the way....
Let us thank God for "VE DAY"!

THE THOUSAND YARD STARE

If I live to be a thousand,
I will never understand....
The odyssey of a soldier's life,
Fighting for one's homeland....

To see men die in battle,
A terrible thing indeed...
To see the wounded suffer,
All crying out in need...!

From shot and shell,
Man's earthly hell....
One prays to God,
The battles to quell....

As bad as this, there's worse to see,
The poor bastards in captivity.....
Men, women, children, all the same,
All subjected to unspeakable pain....

To enter the camp, to set them free,
One can't believe their agony....
The smell of death, all over the place,
The looks of horror on their face....

Imprisoned in wire, spirits broken,
Sadistic guards, crematory fires....
Infestation, humiliation,
Machine gun towers, humanity soured....

Hatred persists, tattoos on wrists,
Privacy gone, striped uniforms....
Stars of David become despised labels,
Starvation reigns, dignity chained....

Jews, Russians, Poles, and the French,
Starved to death, thrown in the trench...
Bodies in heaps, pulled golden teeth,
Desperation thrived, tortured lives...

Through the eyewitness accounts of Mickey Cohen, Div. HQS, 101st Airborne - WWII (see photo), Grif was inspired to put into poetry the chilling accounts of the evidence of Nazi war atrocities against the Jews and others.

Photo taken at the "Airborne Walk" - Fort Benning, Georgia.

Chained to bunks, stagnant air stunk,
Lying in waste, dying in place....
Maggots and flies, children's cries,
Polluted water, missing daughters....!

If I live to be a thousand,
I will never understand...
To be a paratrooper,
To enter no man's land....

To depict such an evil setting,
Still sets my stomach retching.....
To see such evil, men have done,
To see the skeletons, one by one...!

Difficult to tell, the horrors I've seen,
People reduced to pitiful beings....
Enslaved, starved, and murdered,
To please the God-damned Fuhrer...!

Piles of bodies lie everywhere,
Survivors in filth, stench fills the air....
Pitiful beings, I cringed at their touch,
How in the hell, could they suffer so much...!

Men and women, living in fear,
All possessed "The Thousand Yard Stare"...!
Empty eyes, staring in space,
Praying to God, to spare their race...!

If I live to be a thousand,
I will never understand....
What it was to be a child,
To live in no man's land...!

Horror was their way of life,
Terror was their daily strife....
Made to watch their parents die,
All they could do, was scream and cry....!

The children, the poor children,
How they suffered so.....
Life became their nightmare,
Never to outgrow....

Unable to stop the madness,
Limited in what I could do....
I can't erase the image,
The hell that they went through....!

The way their lives were ended,
Leaves mankind most offended....
Horrors endured together,
Tossed in pits, interred forever....!

In a way, the dead are lucky,
For they are quiet now....
God's embrace has stopped their pain,
Heavenly peace is their domain....

Time heals all wounds, so they say,
But they weren't there, to share that day....
Time stands still when hatred reigns,
Scars so deep, can't stop the pain....!

The evil that some men can do,
Haunts other men their whole lives through....
If I live a thousand years,
I will always possess, "The Thousand Yard Stare"

"IVAN'S TOAST"

Let's lift our glasses in the air,
To salute a friend, we hold so dear....
Ivan Worrell is his name,
Our executive secretary, "He's recorded our fame"....

Indian heritage is his beginning,
He can turn defeat, into winning....
His heart is elevated, above the earth,
The eagle, his symbol, from his birth...!

For eight years, he gave us his all,
The end result, we're standing tall....
He took our magazine, gave it a new look,
"The Screaming Eagle", now reads like a book...!

He labored hard, he put it in order,
No association ever had, a better recorder...!
Sometimes his temper had a short fuse,
But his leadership, bound us like glue...!

He made "The Screaming Eagle", what it is today,
A piece of art, "Airborne All The Way"...!
He spread our news, far and wide,
His attitude, "Never Say Die"...!

Our association funds, he kept on track,
Accounting for every dime, he kept us in the black....
Sometimes expenses came out of his pocket,
He refused to let red, reflect on our docket...!

He computerized, our whole organization,
Efficiency is now, our realization...!
Under his guidance, we have grown,
His skill and expertise readily shown...!

Now is the time, we'd like to say,
Ivan, you're "Airborne All The Way"...!
We wish you the best, you've earned our thanks,
"It's going to be tough, to fill your ranks"...!

Ivan is now Editor/Publisher of "The First Screaming Eagles in Vietnam,"
The voice of the 1st Brigade (separate) 1965-68, 101st Abn. Div.

PARATROOPER PADRE

Father Francis L. Sampson, a man of the cloth,
The "Paratrooper Padre", his mission, not a soul lost...!
An elite soldier, who jumped from the sky,
A faithful companion, for ones who might die...!

God created the angels to serve and protect,
He created "Paratrooper Padres" to complete the set....
Saint Michael, the Archangel, an example for all,
Father Sampson, his protege, always standing tall....

The paratrooper's greatest fear,
The Angel of Death, oh so near...!
"Praise the Lord, pass the ammunition,"
An accurate description of the combat condition...!

Hungry, tired, dirty, pushed to the edge,
Praying to God, dodging bullets of lead....
Facing death at every turn,
God's saving grace, the soldier does yearn...!

But there's one comfort, he surely does know,
By his side, the "Paratrooper Padre",
wherever he goes....
Offering encouragement, dispelling confusion,
Comforting the wounded, granting absolution....

A shining example, for all who are near,
This servant of God, showing no fear....
Bursting shells, agonizing yells,
Death's horrible smell, the panic he quells....

The peace of God, he spreads to all,
Saving body and soul, was his call....
His comforting words, his caring touch,
No mortal man, could care as much...!

To dying men, he gave much comfort,
A Christian death, a prayerful tear....
God's embrace, relieved the fear,
All the troopers, knew he cared...!

Braving the hardships, of many a war,
The sacraments of God, he gave to all....
Soldiers loose their fear of death,
Last Rites given, all is forgiven...!

This is the greatest gift, "Paratrooper Padres" can give,
The keys to Heaven, is for the forgiven...!
He patched their bodies, to make them whole,
He risked his life, to save their souls...!

Enduring all that war could give,
To prisoners of war, he gave, the will to live...!
Deprived of all, but their faith,
Father Sampson spread God's saving grace...!

Hearing confessions, saying mass,
Tortured souls, pains that last....
Near starvation, dying of thirst,
Facing atrocities, all the worse...!

Bringing aid and comfort, to soldiers in need,
The sacred Last Rights, the blessed last deed....
To many dying troopers, he put their minds at ease,
Father Sampson turned death, to blessed victory...!

Our "Paratrooper Padre", a man we could kiss,
Served in three wars, no ordinary accomplishment...!
World War II, Korea, and Viet Nam,
To so many lives, he restored the calm...!

Now is the time to say, HOORAY, ...!
To Father Sampson, our "Paratrooper Padre"...!
Thank you sir, for all you've done,
In three wars, OUR HEARTS YOU HAVE WON...!

---

*This poem was inspired by Trooper Mickey Cohen, one of Major General Sampson's
great friends and admirers. Thank you, Mickey, for the information and opportunity
to salute this great man, our "Paratrooper Padre".*
--GRIF

COLONEL ROBERT E. JONES - A SALUTE

Now there is a warrior, there is a man,
A finer soldier, never fought for our land....
He served his country for thirty-three years,
An airborne soldier of the highest tier. . . !

Soldiering was his way of life,
A master blaster, sharp as a knife. . .
Commanding paratroopers was his lot,
Finer soldiers there was not...!

Blazing into Normandy a leader of infantry,
He led his soldiers gallantry ....
Fighting hard, he led the way,
Many Nazi's, now in their graves. . . !

Leaving France to a better fate,
He and his boys, never slowed their gait . . . !
He and his men, of The Strike Force,
Fought like hell and stayed the course... !

Leading his troopers through Rhineland,
The Germans, just couldn't stop his band ....
Jumping in on "Marketgarden",
He and his men, tough and hardened....

Commanding men, such as PFC Joe Mann,
They brought freedom, to the Netherlands ....
Injured while accomplishing this job,
To rest and recuperate he got the nod....

It wasn't long before, he fought in the Korean War,
The Inchon landing, opened that door....
Attacking at the Chosin Reservoir,
The Chinese knew, they'd been gored. . . !

Leading his men in five offensive campaigns,
He left the enemy dead and lame...!
Returning to the United States,
He trained paratroopers, all first rate....

After action reports, of
the highest caliber,
Brought him recogni-
tion and acclaim....
Training manuals,
should bear his name,
He can train, instruc-
tors of war games....

A problem solver, that's first rate,
He can cut, right to the chase...
Razor sharp and full of wit,
He starts off, where others quit. . . !

Assigned as an advisor, in many capacities,
He taught our allies, to fight with tenacity....
Next he commanded the Green Beret,
Then he joined Viet Nam's foray...!

Deputy director, Phoenix Directorate at MACV,
He helped bring the VC, to their knees...!
Rounding out a distinguished career,
He served the colors, loud and clear...!

Now our world is a better place,
Colonel Jones served with dignity and grace...!
Many valor medals adorn his chest,
He's earned his place among the best ...!

Now there's only one thing left to do,
Wish him happiness, his whole life through....
God bless you, Colonel, for what you've done,
You are a legend in the one o' one....!

AIRBORNE!!!!!

Dedicated in honor and respect by your fellow soldiers

DON LASSEN, "MR. AIRBORNE"

Into combat, he took that giant step,
Over Normandy, out of a plane, he leapt....
A paratrooper, with the Five O Five,
"H MINUS", trooper, do or die...!

        A private in the infantry, jumping into infamy,
        One of the boys, who changed history....
        What happened on "D-Day" is no mystery,
        The Cherbourg Peninsula, a drop zone of victory...!

Another combat jump, this time, Holland,
Hitler praying, feverishly and solemn....!
If only "Hell's Highway", as fortified as Arnhem,
Battling allied airborne, certainly, no bargain....

        At "The Battle Of The Bulge", Don, made a change,
        A combat correspondent, he became....
        Writing battle reports, he documented the action,
        A life of journalism, his budding attraction....

After the war, an airborne newsletter, he wrote,
Locating old comrades, never missing their quotes....
Expanding its size, spreading the airborne spirit,
The "Static Line" was born, of journalistic merit....

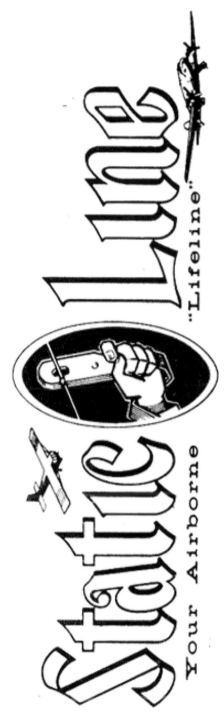

        Over the years, it blossomed and grew,
        All airborne units, now, bound by its glue....
        The Airborne community, enhanced by its news,
        Its pages emit, the red, white and blue...!

Don Lassen has formed, an extensive airborne network,
Its success and excellence, certainly, no quirk....
To sky soldiers, the "Static Line", has immense worth,
Restoring airborne relationships, such satisfying work...

        Don Lassen has earned, a most prestigious title,
        No airborne message, he, ever left to idle....
        He's "Mr. Airborne", staying on tour,
        Spreading Airborne Spirit, his favorite chore....

Reestablishing old friendships, all along the way,
To so many soldiers, he brightens their days....
To keep track of troopers, both old and new,
He fills his hours, so steadfast and true....

        Because of "Mr. Airborne" we never lose touch,
        No Airborne reunion, ever left to luck....
        This is the "Airborne Awards" nineteenth year,
        To "Mr. Airborne", we owe, a hearty salute and cheer...!

God bless you!, Don Lassen, and your "Static Line",
Reading its pages, Airborne's favorite pastime....
Ernie Pyle may have covered more battles than you,
But you are "Mr. Airborne", parachute delivery, right on cue....

LET VALOR NOT FAIL

The 187th Airborne Regimental Combat Team,
One tough, elite, fighting machine....
"The Rakkasans", victorious, time after time,
They have earned, "The Right Of The Line"....

The men who wear the "Steel Beret",
Fought many a battle, saved many a day....
Their baptism by fire, in the Philippines,
Japanese paratroopers, no match,
for this combat team....

At Purple Heart Hill, they caused many a kill,
To enemy soldiers, death, their last thrill....
Jumping into the jungles of Leyte,
Brought an end, to Japanese hey days....

Decisive victories, they gathered at Luzon,
Enemy commanders, wondering, what went wrong...
The Aga Pass led to Tagaytay Ridge,
To the enemy, not an inch they would give....

Manila was a handsome prize,
Mount Macolod, hand to hand fighting,
no compromise...!
Routing the enemy, from bunkers and caves,
To the Philippine people, liberation, they gave....

Shortly after World War II, came to a close,
A strong communist threat, in Korea, arose....
Hordes of enemy soldiers crossed the border,
"Rakkasan Paratroopers", received their orders....

Jumping in at Sukchon and Sunchon, North Korea,
Of AIRBORNE POWER, communists, had no idea....
Annihilating an enemy regiment in the process,
They brought chaos, home to the communists...!

Another combat jump at Munsan-ni,
Heavy fighting resulted in victory....
Cutting enemy supply routes at Uijongbu,
A Chinese withdrawal, so many, they slew...!

Defeating the enemy at every turn,
Communist soldiers, forced to learn....
So confident, at Wonju and Inge,
"The Rakkasans", denied them victory....

Taking on another role,
Communist prisoners, rioting, at Koge do....
The 187 prevented a mass escape,
They slammed the doors, sealing their fate....

In Viet Nam, Rakkasans, played a major role,
Assault helicopters, their way to go....
Fighting hard, in all four corps,
Enemy defeat, a matter of course....

"Hamburger Hill" was a bitter contest,
A North Vietnamese regiment, they laid to rest...
Infiltration routes became unnegotiable,
Communist supplies, became rare and valuable. . . !

This "Nomad Battalion", of Viet Nam,
Bled the enemy, caused much harm....
The "Tet Offensive", a major attack,
Enemy units, sure caught their flak....

The 187, a tough nut to crack,
At Trang Bang, they cut no slack. . .
One of the bloodiest battles of the war,
Killed enemy soldiers, by the scores....

The Ho Bo Woods, the City of Hue,
Defeating the enemy, "All The Way". . . !
At the siege of Khe Sanh,
They proved, oh so strong....

In recent times, they brought peace to the Sinai,
Defused the situation in Lebanon ....
Put tears in Saddam's eyes,
Kuwait set free, with clearer skies....

Over fifty years of decisive victories,
"The Rakkasans", gathered, a most impressive history ..
Many enemies fought, to no avail,
For they live and die their motto,
"LET VALOR NOT FAIL"!!!

*The Author's brother, CPL John T. Griffin was with the "Rakkasans",
when he was KIA two days after parachuting behind enemy lines at Munsan-ni.*

Because of paratroopers such as Dale Duk Foo Yee,
Countless people enjoy a life that's free......
His personal combat, fought in the Philippines,
He helped shatter, that Japanese, ruthless scheme....

The Japanese military was fulfilling their dreams,
Conquering a people, slavery and torture, their means.....
Many innocent people were to die,
So many missing, no markers, where they lie.....

Because of troopers, such as Private Dale Yee,
Many survived, to relate their hellish story.....
Los Baños, a prison camp, a hell on earth,
Caused so many people, to curse their birth......

Life under such conditions, not fit for a dog,
Horrible sufferings, not recorded or logged.....
It was never meant to be known,
Their misery, torture, rapes, names left unknown....

Praying to God, prisoners sought refuge,
Dignity gone, only hope, left to lose......
To many, death was a blessing,
Diseases, infections, no bandages or dressings.....

God in his mercy, offered a way,
Brave paratroopers would save the day.....
Dale was one, of only a hundred and thirty,
To undertake this mission, a mission of mercy....

"An Impossible Mission", this "Liberation at Dawn"
Behind enemy lines, nothing must go wrong!
Six thousand enemy saturated the area,
They must strike fast, cause enemy hysteria...!

Jump in, free the prisoners, be on their way,
Accomplishing the mission, they made history that day....
These paratroopers saved thousands of souls,
The devil cursing, in his hell far below.....

Wounded in combat, Dale helped finish the task,
A free Philippines, liberation at last......
Dale's story, of Paratroopers, daring and bold,
Their valorous deeds will never grow old.......

Now Editor of the "Airborne Quarterly"
Dale invites you to tell your story.......
You and your Airborne Spirit must live on,
So many battles, what's your Luzon?....

PARATROOPER DALE YEE - A SALUTE

With much affection and respect!
by Peter Griffin and Mickey Cohen

A RELUCTANT HERO

In the Army, it is yours, to do or die,
You never question, the reasons why....
A young soldier, in World War II,
Full of doubt, but he'll see it through....

He trained in artillery, he taught at Fort Sill,
He became a master, of that skill....
Thinking he had found his niche,
Unprepared, for a change, so quick....

Ordered to Officer Candidate School,
Uneducated, he didn't have the tools....
Given no choice, he was forced to attend,
In the top ten of his class, he did end....

Now an officer and gentleman,
Oh so reluctantly, he settled in....
Always, always, so afraid of heights,
No worry, in the artillery, he'd be all right.....

BUT- he received a new assignment,
Reluctantly, he was forced to try it...
Into airborne gliders, he was ordered,
Is there no end, to his torture ?

The glider, roped, behind the plane,
Knowing certain death, would end his pain...!
The glider lifted off, before the plane...!
To hell with this, he'd face the shame...!

"Pilot, land this thing, or I'll shoot you!"
Rather be a live coward, than a dead fool...
The pilot shouted, "It is too late!"
Reluctantly, he hung on, forced to accept his fate....

A "Screaming Eagle" he became,
Swearing, he'd never jump from a plane....
A good artillery job, his only need,
BUT- along with it an eagle to feed...!

"Old Abe", the 101st precious mascot,
To care for it, he knew not....
Not knowing what an eagle ate,
He ordered his cook, to prepare its plates....

Passing the buck, he'd be okay,
Until that awful, dreaded day....
"The eagles dead, on its back, feet in the air,
Never had he known, such terrible fear...!

"Report to the General, right away!",
Knowing a court martial, was headed his way...!
Not a word about the eagle was made,
General McAuliffe asked him, to be his aide...!

Silently thanking, his loving God,
Fearful, not to accept the job....
Hurry, bury the eagle, mark its grave,
Ordered to England, HE WAS SAVED...!

Then, those dreaded words, he heard the General say,
WE ARE going to jump today...!
Reluctantly, caught in another snare,
Jumped from the plane, so ill prepared...!

He and the General, shared a room,
Wasn't long, their friendship bloomed....
General McAuliffe, a gentleman, so fine,
Taught him much, he always found time....

The General never uttered a profane word,
But "Nuts!" was often, clearly heard....
If something was going astray,
"Nuts!", meant correct it! He would not sway...

Meeting Eisenhower, Bradley, Patton, and Montgomery,
They made their way, all over that country....
Learning much, as he went,
Not an idle minute, was ever spent....

To Normandy, they made their way,
As an air observer, he earned his pay....
To find the enemy, he must take to the sky,
Knowing, any minute, they'd crash and die....

Coaching the pilot, all was well,
Careful, careful, we're doing swell....
"Enemy fire, enemy fire!", he did yell,
Fear of heights, "Nuts!, dive like hell"....

Finally, safety, duty on the ground,
As forward observer, he'd be safe and sound...!
BUT- dodging bullets, he'd stoop and sway,
If he spotted the enemy, he'd make them pay...!

Totally exhausted, too tired to bitch,
Joined three soldiers, asleep in a ditch...
Just a blanket, to make his bed,
He fell asleep, AMONGST THE DEAD...!

Operation Market Garden was the next show,
From England, across the channel, again, our hero did go
This time in a glider under tow,
Wouldn't you know, one of its windows did blow....

Over the water, he looked down,
Great warships were all around....
The glider damaged, the pilot suggested, "they cut loose",
"HELL NO!, I CAN'T SWIM!, I'LL SURELY DROWN"'

Despite being ripped open,
the glider touched down near Nijmegen,
Enemy shells exploding all around them ... !
Hurriedly, they ran for cover into some woods,
Have to unload the "sawed off" howitzer later, readily
understood...

"Hell's Highway" was just a narrow road,
Two way traffic, two large trucks, it couldn't hold....
"Bottlenecks" all over the place,
Of the British column there wasn't a trace...

Ordered to find them, our hero snatched a Jeep,
Evading the Germans, he'd bound and leap....
Finally he located the late British column,
Having tea!, their custom, quite proper and solemn...

Near Eindhoven, he set up artillery on the "Island",
Of the Germans, t'was not hard to find them ... !
Soaking pup tents, little sleep, mud a foot deep,
Sucked his jump boots right off his feet...

After heavy fighting in Holland, they finished their job,
Off to Belgium, they did trod....
Hitler had started, a daring attack,
At Bastogne, he'd drive the allies back...

Here the 101st would make their stand,
At all costs, they must hold this land...!
Fighting hard, in the bitter cold,
A major push, could they still hold...?

A heavy fog had settled in,
Hitler's generals, sure they'd win...
The paratroopers, low on supplies and ammunition,
Their reinforcements could not break in....

The Nazi brass, sent a delegation,
"Surrender now or face annihilation!"
General McAuliffe replied with "Nuts!"
He wondered if, they were out of luck...

The Nazis responded with horrific barrages,
Enemy infantry made savage charges....
The "Screaming Eagles" were holding their ground,
He fired his howitzers, at enemy sounds....

For in the dense fog, no one could see,
An enemy regiment, dug in, under some trees...!
Causing havoc, inflicting much pain,
Our infantry attacks, all ended in vain....

He ordered his artillery, to fire air bursts,
Then this enemy, suffered their worst....
Bracketing fire, rained death and destruction,
Their screams were heard, without obstruction...!

Sweeping fire, back and forth,
Repeating it, as a matter of course....
Finally, lifting his deadly fire,
Without resistance, HIS WOODS, were reacquired...!

Then the fog cleared, the skies so blue,
Parachutes came, just floating through...!
Delivering precious supplies and ammunition,
Ending their very desperate condition...!

When the battle was finally done,
A great victory had been won
Bastogne survived a terrible siege,
The 101st had held, until relieved!

For Hitler it was, the beginning of the end,
Never to amass, such armies again...
They retreated across the Rhine,
Their swastikas covered in blood and grime...!

Now you're all wondering, who this could be
This silent contributor to victory....
In stature, he is just a little man,
But you'll need a ladder, to shake his hand....

Captain Vincent Vicari is his name,
He's given much, to the 101st fame....
Anonymous, he'd prefer to be,
A RELUCTANT HERO, lost in the pages of history....

But Captain, a living monument, you are,
You surpassed, what is considered par....
Now we all know, just what you've done,
A RELUCTANT HERO of the One o' One...!

Photo courtesy of Joe Quade, Editor "Thunder from Heaven" 17th A/B

FOR LOVE OF FAMILY

I was blessed, to come to know a man,
A man whose philosophy, was simply, "I can"...
A man who led an extraordinary life,
A man who stood for, what is right....

Of Chinese origin, he became an American,
Respected his roots, loved his new land ....
Honoured his parents, learned by example,
Always worked hard, his body, supple and ample....

Strong enough, to meet any task,
Need a favor? Simply, just ask....
A truer friend, one could never meet,
A friendly word, to all he'd greet....

As a young man, he fought in war,
A patriot, to his very core. . .
Became a paratrooper, brave and elite,
He accomplished, near impossible feats....

A member of the 11th Airborne Division,
He fought to save lives, under the worst conditions...
In the Philippines, be battled in jungles,
To America's enemies, he brought much trouble....

American civilian prisoners, he helped set free,
To Los Baños prison camp, jumping in,
he provided the key ....
An impossible mission, ended triumphantly,
Two thousand plus souls, celebrated life and liberty....

Left:
Dale Yee (right) with close friend James B. King taking part in memorial ceremonies at San Joaquin National Cemetery, CA. (Feb. 1996)
King and members of his unit, 457 Parachute Field Artillery, provided covering fire as the liberated prisoners from Los Baños Prison evacuated, escorted by troopers of the 11th Airborne.

Top photo:
Dale Yee with wife, Roberta and #3 son, Challen (Sept. 1965).

Grievously wounded, fighting the Japanese,
He helped free, the Philippines....
He would always remember, through tearful eyes,
His brother troopers, who gave their lives....

A man of duty, honor, country,
A man who earned all he achieved...
Love of God, brought him to his knees,
Also Roberta, the girl of his dreams...

In proposal, he pledged his love,
Bonded perfect, like hand and glove.
Throughout life, her love she'd give
In perfect harmony, they did live...

They were blessed, their children numbered four,
Each one loved, cherished, and adored ....
They taught them, the values of family life,
Of God, decency, respect, and other's rights....

As a family, they embraced community,
As a family, they celebrated God's divinity...
Setting an example, for all to see,
Shared their blessings, with all in need....

Education, always of great importance,
Friendly advice? You need no appointment....
They hold their neighbors, in great esteem,
To them, brotherhood, "The American Dream"....

For the gift, he gave, to you and me,
Is the gift, of his legacy....
DUTY, HONOR, COUNTRY,
He did it all, FOR LOVE OF FAMILY....

Of Whom I speak, is Dale F. Yee,
The founder of "Airborne Quarterly"....
I, for one, will never forget,
Reading his pages, I've laughed and wept....

In Dale's life, he touched us all,
For all of us, he answered his call....
A blessing to our Airborne community,
For brothers-at-arms, FOR LOVE OF FAMILY...

**Proud as an eagle, LTG. Joseph M. Swing, commander of the 11th Airborne Division (WWII), stands with statue honoring the 11th Airborne. Statue was created by Bill Porteous, 11th A/B.
Units of General Swing's division played keys roles in the successful liberation of the Los Baños Prison Camp in Luzon, Philippines, with its over 2100 civilian prisoners of war on 23 February 1945.
Dale Yee (opposite page) jumped with Company B-511, who were assigned as the main airborne assault force.
The remarkable success of the rescue operation is attributed to detailed intelligence, outstanding execution of recon and diversion units, the exigent manner by which allied commanders acted in effort to protect innocent lives. No allied casualties resulted from the assault on the prison camp in what is known as "The Liberation at Dawn".**

War, so tragic, in many ways,
How to plan life, day by day ....
To wait for someone, in harm's way,
Is tomorrow, my last day .... ?

     I could not ask, you wait for me,
     Separated by more, than just a sea ....
     To pledge my love, on bended knee,
     Knowing my life, be in jeopardy ....

I looked for your letters every day,
The war dragged on endlessly ....
Then the word, came from you,
You fell in love, we were through ....

I will always love you...

     My lost love, how I miss your tenderness,
     Your memory, My only happiness .....
     Your sweet memory, etched in my heart,
     There, you belong to me, never to part ....

For memories are, all that remain,
Not meant to be, you share my name ....
Beautiful days and romantic nights,
Gone forever, not to fill my life ....

     True love comes, but once in life,
     A broken heart, my perpetual plight .....
     Condemned to sadness, my whole life through,
     Eternal loneliness, in place of you .....

Oh so long, since I've seen your face,
Much too long, since I felt your embrace ....
Oh so long, since your lips, I've kissed,
Much too long, your love I've missed .....

     So sadly, life, beyond our control,
     By hurting people, we injure our souls ....
     Is life destined, forever to be,
     Love for others, not for me .... ?

So long ago, out hearts entwined,
We shared a love, so sublime ....
Tragically, a love, not meant to be,
For then, I could not belong to thee .....

     Now, life has changed, the war has passed,
     Your love given, your die, been cast ....
     Your name, now changed, shouts aloud,
     Telling me, beware, I dare not crowd ....

So my love, forever, I'll be gone,
In your life, forsaken, I don't belong ....
As I close, be sure you know,
Wherever you go, my heart will follow ....

I will always love you .... dear, John

Valentines Day, 1946

HUE AND CRY

In October, 1951, a HUE AND CRY, went unheard,
Of atomic blasts, our government, longed to learn....
So it came to be, soldiers, used, in atomic testing,
The human tragedy, be still unfolding....

Obedient soldiers, all were they,
Under strict orders, none would stray....
883 men, all trapped, no way out,
Over time, ailments and death, would result .....

All of them, every Mother's son,
In the Nevada desert, cooked, till done....
"Operation Buster/Jangle", it was named,
U.S. Paratroopers, thrown, into a deadly game....

To what benefit, could this serve?,
To illuminate, a human's every nerve ... ?
Guinea pigs, forced, they would become,
Perform, they would, for the country they loved....

The war in Korea, was still raging,
Chinese communists, all fronts, staging....
Atomic bombs, to be used, in close support,
Total annihilation, the last resort...?

Was this the reason, unheard, the HUE AND CRY?,
Whatever the risk?, our soldiers, "to do and die" ....
Be they just fodder, to use at government will....?
For a better way, to maim and kill.... !

These soldiers, not provided, any protective gear,
The government said, "you have nothing to fear ....
To your health, exposure, will have no effect,
Any danger, we'll surely detect"...!

These soldiers, exposed to seven detonations,
Did not share, the government's exhilaration .....
Ordered to "Police", after each equation,
All were subjected to contamination...!

"Camp Desert Rock", certainly, no place to be,
Ionizing-radiation exposure, not a victory....
Life was at extremely high risk,
None of these Paratroopers, had a death wish....

The government constructed, several "Doom Towns"
Amongst the buildings, animals were bound .....
Sheep, goats, dogs and pigs, caught in the blast,
Seared to death, with their last gasp...

"Ground Zero", where the bomb exploded,
A place where courage and valor, could be eroded....
Never the less, these soldiers had to go,
Through these "Tulips", soldiers, couldn't tiptoe...

Just one bomb, detonated on November 1st,
Equaled the bombing, that sealed Nagasaki's fate:...
In just minutes, soldiers, at "Ground Zero",
Not a single one, ever called "HERO"...!

Compensation made, to civilians down wind,
When will "Atomic Vets", JUST DUES begin .... ?
Devastating health problems, plague their lives,
Pain stabs their bodies, like a knife .... !

Over 20% fathered children with genetic defects,
The government claims, no radiation effects....
If politicians born, such daughters and sons,
Damned straight, something, would soon be done....

You, the American people, please, NOW, hear their HUE AND CRY,
For it was for you, they risked their lives....
Our government, recklessly, put them in harm's way,
They need your voice, to save the day .... !

The Veterans Administration, surely then, would address their needs....
Your strong voice, our government, would heed .... !
Your HUE AND CRY, would bring just compensation,
Finally, they would experience, their exhilaration ... !"

THE PURPOSE OF THIS POEM IS TO BRING TO THE PUBLIC'S ATTENTION THE PLIGHT OF MANY OF OUR
BRAVE "ATOMIC VETERANS" AND THEIR FAMILIES...
MAY GOD BLESS THEM AND "GOD BLESS AMERICA!"

THIS POEM IS DEDICATED WITH HONOR AND RESPECT TO ALL ATOMIC VETERANS.
GOD BLESS YOU FOR YOUR BRAVE SERVICE TO OUR COUNTRY. IT IS MY PROFOUND
HOPE THAT YOU BE FINALLY RECOGNIZED FOR YOUR MOST HONORABLE SERVICE. I
HOPE THEY AWARD YOU THE "NUCLEAR RADIATION MEDAL", YOU SO DESERVE...

In loving memory of my brother,
PFC William J. Griffin, Jr.
Aged 57 years
Co. A, 1st Battalion, 188th Infantry Regiment
11th Airborne Division (1951)

MUCH MORE
THAN YOU AND I

Battles fought, the physical pain is over,
So many friends, asleep, beneath the clover...
Warriors all, they stood so tall,
Blood soaked ground, solemn Taps, sound their call...

Memories of heroes past,
They dared to breathe, their precious last......
We are free, for they stood fast,
Their death grip, LIBERTY, in their grasp.....

All their efforts, sacrifices, not in vain,
"Uncle Sam" bears no shame.......
The torch of liberty, bears no strain,
Our fallen warriors, the glow of her eternal flame......

All, our brothers, oh, so many names,
Their personal courage, "Old Abe's" fame...
Let's salute, those who dared to die,
Those who gave, MUCH MORE THAN YOU AND I....

YOUR NAMES ENGRAVED

On Good Friday, March 23rd , 1951,
A major Airborne assault, had begun....
145 combat cargo planes, filled the sky,
Thousands of communists, about to die....

3,300 troopers of the 187th Airborne
Regimental Combat Team,
Did "hit the silk", each man, lean and mean....
Hitting the ground, their weapons readied,
Their enemy, 20,000 strong, there was a plenty....

Behind the Paratroopers, came the heavy drops,
The 674th Field Artillery, battle ready, completed the lot...
A first, this jump, made Airborne history,
But would "Operation Tomahawk", end in victory .... ?

Landing south of Munsan-ni, nine miles from North Korea,
Behind enemy lines, could they fulfill this panacea...?
After securing the vast drop zone,
Fight, then advance, they set their tone....

For two bloody days, they kept this pitch,
Always in the open, no cover, nary a ditch
Fight, hurry, reach Uijongbu, cut the enemy supply route,
Rain, wet ground, heavy, muddy, sloshing, jump boots....

Day break, Easter Sunday, secure the hill ahead,
The cost, be much blood and dead....
In a horizontal formation, they moved out,
Crossing flat land, they suspected, a gory bout...

All of the sudden, all hell broke out,
Came swarms of enemy, "charge",
in Chinese, they did shout....
For awhile, the "Rakkasans", held their own,
Just too many bastards, how their numbers had grown .....

Swinging and firing. "burp guns", from the hip,
Troopers falling, "slap, slap," as they were hit ....
Deadly enemy fire, slowing their advance,
"Keep moving forward", must take the chance .....

The 187 opened up with a roar,
Killing Chinese, by the score....
But still, troopers fell, with moans and shrieks,
Such depleted ranks, their outlook bleak .... !

This bloody place, called Parun-ni,
Many a soldier, faced eternity .....
Not able to advance, nor retreat,
Suddenly artillery, boom, boom, repeat, repeat....

The enemy dispersed and scurried away,
The 674th had saved the day .... !
For a few moments, they caught their breath,
Not enough time, to eat or rest....

It rained, again, as the "Rakkasans" counter-attacked,
Avenging soldiers, they'd offer no slack .....
The enemy dead, piled up before them,
Enemy strength, no longer a quorum .....

187th ARCT makes low level jump in first attack wave at Munsan-ni, Korea, March 23, 1951.

Chasing the Chinese, up and over, the objective,
Now, total annihilation, the enemy, would be subjective...
To their front, loomed, another great hill,
Reaching its peak, they set up the kill .....

It's a mountain! as they surveyed that rise,
A large land mass, met their eyes.... !
With such depleted ranks, could they hold them back?
To their despair, bugles sounded a full attack .... !

The entire rise, covered by charging Chinese,
Grey swarms, as far, as the eye could see ....
Wave after wave, the enemy attacked,
By sheer numbers, they'd break their backs .....

With "Rakkasan" backs, thrown, against the wall,
Out of ammo, rifles swinging, many did fall....
Others firing their 45's, desperately, trying to stay alive,
Now facing, their annihilation, would any survive .... ?

Suddenly, support companies were on the scene,
Laying down murderous fire, heard the enemy scream....
Dropping their "burp guns",
leaving their wounded and their dead,
Suffered much, as they fled...

This is how Easter Sunday came to an end,
As "Rakkasans" gathered their injured and dead....
Down the hill, a priest is saying mass,
Survivors joined in, to the last....

After Service, finally, eating hot C's,
Soothing hot coffee, easing many a worry .....
But then came the order, "move it out",
Enough strength left for another bout ... ?

Heading back towards Munsan-ni,
Hills 519 and 322, entrenched, a hidden enemy....
As the paratroopers, scaled these mountains,
Mortars and machine guns, pounded them....

Over their heads, swish, swish, swish,
The 674th granting, yet another wish .....
The deadly mortars and guns, now silent,
The sounds of digging, becoming most evident....

At the top of these mountains, boot high snow,
By aerial observation, an entrenched enemy,
clearly showed....
The paratroopers attacked, facing strong resistance,
Despite casualty, after casualty, they went the distance....

Finally, after much blood, carnage and death,
The 234th Chinese Regiment, was laid to rest....
The surviving troopers, now realizing, they had won,
To North Korea, retreating communists, on the run....

Catching them withdrawing, in an open ravine,
"Rakkasan" machine guns created a gory scene....
Destroying an entire army of North Korean and Chinese,
Total victory was achieved .... !

Many of the "Steel Berets", had met their fate,
But quick to reach, Saint Peter's Gates....
As God welcomed these heroes inside,
You could hear him cry....

To you heroes, who did survive,
This horrific battle, just won't subside .....
But be it known, you have earned your place,
Your comrades await, your presence, inside the gates .....

The highest entity, did not forget your war,
As you know, he's been keeping score....
To his angels, he sings your praise,
In his book of the faithful, YOUR NAMES ENGRAVED .....

THAT RUSTING CRATE

Orders were cut, the men well trained,
The 1st Brigade of 101st Airborne fame ...
3700 Paratroopers, all hand picked,
To Viet Nam, they'd soon be shipped ....

In early July of 1965,
At Oakland Terminal, we did arrive ....
Thoughts of combat, we had surmised,
But not the hulk, that met our eyes ....

"Donut Dollies", cheerfully, gave us their wares,
As if to lessen, our growing fears ....
Donuts and coffee, not enough to relieve,
Life on land, we'd soon grieve ....

Moored to the dock, the
"USNS GENERAL LEROY ELTINGE",
On THAT RUSTING CRATE our lives would hinge ...
A mothballed troopship, of years gone by,
Crossing on it, would we survive .... ?

Was it seaworthy? would it stay afloat?,
Drowned in saltwater, our bodies would bloat ....
All envisioned a watery grave,
Against a shark, could you be brave?

Only 510 feet from bow to stern,
Of personal space, all would yearn ....
Fighting the crowd, to get to a rail,
Bumping each other, like cows corralled ....

Moored in place, for two long nights,
Staring at the city's lights ....
San Francisco, a great place to be,
But California, we had not come to see ....

Finally, we were underway,
Passing Alcatraz, along the way ....
Then, under the Golden Gate, we passed,
Wondering, how long, this voyage, to last .... ?

Entering the Pacific, oh so blue,
Thousands of jellyfish, of many hues ....
Flying fish led the way,
From this prison, none would stray ....

Chowlines ringed the ship, all the long day,
Standing at tables, we ate that way ....
As soldiers regurgitated, in their trays,
The swaying of ship, slid it your way ....

Saltwater showers, soap, no lather,
On the decks, friends, struggled, to gather ....
On THAT RUSTING CRATE, there were no latrines ...
"Oh My God", I heard someone scream ... !

Sweltering holes, in the bowels of the ship,
Personal space, just did not exist ....
Stacked four high, on canvass cots,
Swaying of sea, stomachs in knots ....

The man above you, empties his guts,
Drenched in vomit, just your luck ....
Wiping yourself, with your last towel,
Thanking God, it be not, his bowels ....

Everyday , they broke up fights,
Hoping no one, pulled a knife ....
Quarters too cramped, nerves too frayed,
To keep the peace, our Chaplains prayed ...

Boredom became everyone's enemy,
Gambling, not considered obscenity ....
Not much to do, see or read,
A fight or two, to make them bleed ...

One day, all fought for the rails,
Excitement!, the carcass of a whale ....
In its center, a huge, bloody crater,
Feeding Albatrosses, was "Mother Nature"....

Across the ocean, we plodded along,
Of Terra Firma, we did long ....
Ten long days and nights, at sea,
No gravy, in this damned navy ... !

There was no laundry, on the boat,
We tied our fatigues, to a rope ....
Across the water, they would skip,
Saltwater stained, as they dripped ....

No room at the bow, but ... we attempted PT,
Like the Macarena, barely, could touch our knees ....
By the numbers, one, two, three, four,
"Tell the people, what she wore"....

Only peanut brittle, sold at the ship's store,
Boxes of Peco's Pete, we did hoard ....
"Crunch, crunch, crunch", became an annoying sound,
One more bite, we'd go twelve rounds ...

On clear nights, a movie, some saw,
Only a small unit, could answer that call ....
Too many men, for all to see,
A sudden downpour, our first fatality ...

A trooper asleep, on a lower deck,
The stairwell crowded, getting wet ....
Unknowingly, a soldier leapt,.
Landing full force, crushing his chest ...

No space, so into the brig, his body went,
No air conditioning to purge deaths scent ....
Suddenly all was quiet, not a sound,
The engines failed, our hearts did pound ...

For a solid day, we were adrift,
Prayed for something, anything, to give us a lift ....
Finally, the crew, got us underway,
Another prayer, to keep us going our way ....

Into Subic Bay, for repairs and rest,
They docked the ship, three abreast ....
Ashore for just two hours, but it was swell,
Enough to down, some San Miguels ....

Our casualty disembarked with prayers,
As mechanics completed, much needed repairs ....
Never had I seen a place so green,
As we said "goodbye", to the Philippines ....

Only two days from Cam Ranh Bay,
New anxieties, came our way ....
Can you kill? are you prepared to die ... ?
"Ours is but to do or die, not ours to reason, WHY?"

One day out, miraculously, the struggling stopped,
For each other, suddenly, we cared a lot ....
On that ship, a band of brothers, we became,
Calling each other, by first names ....

Suddenly, a fighter plane, flew by,
Tilting its wings, a welcoming, "Hi"....
An immediate bond, to other military branches,
The NVA would fight, all our lances ...

Excitedly! someone shouted, "LAND!",
Of mountainous jungles, palms and sand ....
As evening fell, "The Eltinge" docked,
Reality! Viet Nam, now our lot ....

THAT RUSTING CRATE, now a refuge, one last night,
Concussion grenades, boomed, to morning light ....
Into a hostile land, we disembarked, to meet our fate,
A sentimental, "GOODBYE" to
THAT RUSTING CRATE ... !

This poem was inspired by my good friend and a great soldier,
JIM SOPRANO, one of the "Boat People." - Grif

"DAKTO, A LESSON FOR ME AND YOU"...

In June of 1966, two deadly forces would converge,
An all out battle, the blood would surge...
The 101st Airborne and the 24th NVA,
They'd lock their horns, those fateful days.....

General Giap ordered the mission,
"Annihilate the American forces at Dakto....
Destroy them all, their base camps too,
No one left alive, when you're through....!"

Over the hills of Toumorong they swarmed,
To silence our guns, not forewarned....
Attacking from all four sides,
Our listening posts, caught by surprise....

These outposts spread the news,
As enemy rounds slid down their tubes...
As the sentinels were overrun,
The strengthening of defenses had begun....

The 326th Engineers had constructed, a vital bridge,
Fighting as infantry, heroically,
not an inch they would give...!
Later under heavy fire, in triple canopy,
they cut out LZ's,
Evacuating our wounded, relieving their suffering...

Whistles blowing, machine guns glowing,
Mortar blasts, wounded groaning.....
Charging our howitzers by cover of dark,
Bee Hive rounds, finding their mark....!

Green tracers lit up the sky,
Charlie shouting, "Tonight you die".....
Captured radios, Charlie on our wire,
Army vehicles exploding in fire....

Grenades being thrown, satchels are blown,
Fix bayonets, hold your own.....
M16's in full roar, enemy khaki, a bloody gore,
105's firing at point blank, decimating enemy ranks....

"Puff the Magic Dragon" flies over the hill,
Firing mini guns, multiplying the kills.....
"Smokey the Bear" dropping their flares,
Enemy confusion, seen quite clear.......

When daylight comes, we attack in great force,
But Charlie had run, enough for this course....
Not much time to catch our breath,
Refitting ourselves, we went after our catch.....

Our Tiger Force, hunting in the valley,
Attacked a strong force that had rallied......
Out numbered and outgunned,
The Tigers chewed 'em up, but were badly stung....

The North Vietnamese Army was finding out,
Just what Airborne soldiers were all about.....
Never had so few, been so tough to chew,
Thinking they'd won, our hunting, just begun.....

Charlie Company of the O' deuce
Was prowling on the loose.....
Catching a large force by surprise,
The enemy decided, "Must do or die"!

Encircling our force on "No Name Ridge",
The NVA charged, no quarter they'd give.....
Tightening the belt, stealing our breath,
"Napalm our position, or we face certain death"....

The enemy intent on zeroing them out,
Devastating this unit, would begin their rout....
Knowing relief would be forthcoming,
Swarms of enemy soldiers started buzzing....

Abu Company of the 1st 327,
Rushed to their aid, a force sent from heaven.....
Dropping all caution, to proceed like the wind,
The NVA set deadly traps, to insure their win.....

Camouflaged bunkers already in place,
An L-shaped ambush would seal Abu's fate...
AK's opened up with a roar,
Charlie was quick to slam the door.....

Two units now trapped, they poised for the kill,
Licking their lips, enjoying the thrill.....
Only one thing stood in the way,
Only Airborne courage, could save the day....!

Fighting hard, for all their worth,
Supporting fires shook the earth.....
These Paratroopers kept counterattacking,
To survive, they must have backing.....

They gathered their wounded and made a stand,
Repulsing the enemy, at times, hand to hand....
Rain and darkness shrouded the land,
The enemy started probing, showing their plan....

The blessed darkness was a gift,
The enemy soldiers could not persist....!
As quiet as possible we left our enclave,
Carrying our wounded, our withdrawal was made....

It wouldn't be long before we knew,
A mighty arc light would strike from the blue....
Great craters erupted throughout the jungle,
The sanctuary of the NVA, reduced to rubble.....

This North Vietnamese Army was rendered unfit
These brave Screaming Eagles refused to quit...
Badly outnumbered they evened the odds,
Securing the area, they finished their job.....

The Battle of Dak To was a very vicious fight,
Both sides lost much of their might....
Lessons were learned at a very high price,
A drop of blood would only pay for a grain of rice...!

The bravery of our badly outnumbered men,
Defeated a determined enemy at the end....
Leaders such as
Emerson, Hackworth, Brown and Carpenter,
Greatly bettered the odds and prevented our slaughter....

Anticipating General Giap's devilish traps,
"Gunfighter" taught him a lesson on counterattack....
Defeating the enemy on their own sod,
The 24th North Vietnamese Army was reduced
to a squad...!

This poem is humbly dedicated to LTG Henry E. Emerson (Ret),
"Gunfighter", our beloved battalion commander. His gallant leadership
and courage on the battlefield is only surpassed by his affection for the
men of his "STRIKE FORCE". Sir, please know our respect and love for
you will never "FADEAWAY"! God Bless You, Sir. "Grif"

SAIGON TEA

Long ago, in a faraway land,
American soldiers, ordered, to lend a hand....
Communist aggression taking place,
Must help our allies, to save their face....

To preserve democracy, in South Viet Nam,
Our young soldiers, take up arms....
They must stop the Viet Cong, and NVA,
Communist soldiers, must be made to pay....

Freedom must blossom, under the royal palm,
Impoverished peasants, forced to pay alms....
Montaguards, primitive people, forced into slavery,
They became our allies, fought so bravely....

Months of fighting, under jungle canopy,
Exhausted witness, so much calamity....
Young warriors get a much needed rest,
Off to Saigon, "Pearl of the Orient"....

Beautiful young girls for five hundred P,
Just keep their glass, full of SAIGON TEA....
"You love me, I love you, OK?,"
Not much pleading, the soldier will stay...!

How awful, what war will do,
Naive young people, used, through and through....
Innocent young girls, trapped in despair,
Plunged into decadence, such pretty black hair....

Young soldiers and whores, fill Tudo Street,
Slowly transformed none no longer, young or sweet....
War and black markets, take their tolls,
Leaving black marks on many young souls....

To see so much death, life, made so cheap,
Young people become, ugly black sheep....
The horrors of war PASS OVER, no doors,
Life is corrupted, mutilated , by scores....

Back to the war, kill or be killed,
Tired, sick, so much blood spilled ....
Lull in the fighting, must relieve the stress,
Back to the girl, in the tight dress....

The Tan Loc Hotel, is the place to go,
American music, blended whiskey ....
There's Madame Trang, you feel so lame,
Oh so tired, of the killing game....

She's been reduced, to a prostitute,
Once a GOOD girl, made destitute.....
War and poverty, took a very high toll,
She prays to God, to save body and soul....

Your tour is up, your war is over,
Back to the States, to a life of clover...
How can this be, you're so unhappy, life is misery,
No peace of mind, alcohol becomes your therapy.....

You can't forget, the innocence lost,
So unprepared, to pay the cost....
Just didn't know, what it would do to me,
The price of war, and SAIGON TEA...

NVA - North Vietnamese Army   SAIGON TEA- shot glass of tea
Whiskey price - 1 Piasters (P)   VN money - 120 P = 1 U.S. dollar

HAWTHORNE'S HILL

At dusk an eight man patrol, made its way,
At Tuy Hoa, the 101st Airborne, would save the day....
To protect the rice harvest, orders were cut,
Feeding South Vietnam's population, a must....

Every year, the Viet Cong, stole the crop,
ARVN and ROK marines, the pillage, couldn't stop....
So the 2/502nd Infantry, given the task,
They would accomplish, all that was asked....

The patrol assigned, to start the mission,
Swarm of mosquitoes, worsened conditions....
Through rivers, jungles, and paddies,
Enemy territory, much like Hades....

Sgt. Gene Hawthorne, the patrol leader,
To engage the enemy, was most eager....
An American Indian, adept at tracking,
His skills and experience, was not lacking....

In jungle so thick, visibility, minimal,
Heard the VC, stealthy, as animals....
Screaming and shooting, the enemy attacked,
The patrol exploding, cut no slack....

The enemy fell, wave after wave,
Was a foolish tactic, they engaged....
The patrol suffered, one man killed,
In close combat, all were skilled....

The enemy withdrew, a blood trail, leaving,
A booby trap exploded, one dead,
Sgt. Hawthorne bleeding....
At dawn, the enemy, attacked again,
The six soldiers remaining, sent them reeling....

Sgt. Hawthorne, bled profusely, badly hurt,
Still he fought, for all his worth....
He called in the artillery, accurate and deadly,
The large enemy force, suffered a plenty....

The patrol held, till we arrived,
The remaining six, had survived....
Sgt. Hawthorne, to a medevac, carried away,
"Need blood, give me a refill, can I stay ?"

After many firefights, we completed the mission,
The 95th NVA Regiment, bleeding and hungry,
now their condition...
After two weeks of fighting, we passed, HAWTHORNE'S HILL,
The enemy still lay, where they were killed....

The nauseating smell of death, did permeate,
A most macaberesque scene, my mind, still recreates....
Thirty-five dead VC, fermenting, where they lay,
I can't forget, the horror they displayed ... !

Flies and maggots, their job complete,
Skeletons, with a tar-like substance, did secrete ....
One skull lay atop a ditch,
Its body, rolled down the bank, covered in pitch ....

The other skeletons, lay all about,
"Please bury me," I could hear them shout...
Weapons gone, but fully dressed,
This vivid vision, I can't suppress...

Of bones and tar, they did stink,
A most appalling odor, they did reek....
To their skeletons, their gear still attached,
Ho Chi Minh sandals, to bones, held fast....

The blackened sockets, that once held eyes,
Still glare at me, no tears to cry....
I tell you all this, so you can see,
In war and death, be a tragic reality....

Though, on HAWTHORNE'S HELL, I did not fight,
Of heroism and horrors, in dreams, my plight....
From an uneasy sleep, I jolt awake,
From this nightmare, there's no escape...

Sgt. Hawthorne recovered, valor, heroism, gallantry, his traits,
But at Nhon Cho, in a Chinook, he met his fate....
Full of ammunition, it exploded, in a ball of fire,
Burnt beyond recognition, 21 heroes, their lives expired....

In an unpopular war, many heroes did fight,
So in pleasant, safe sleep, you spend your nights....
Combat veterans, don't have that luxury,
Too many a HAWTHORNE'S HILL,
to haunt their memories....

ARVN - ARMY REPUBLIC OF VIET NAM   ROK - REPUBLIC OF KOREA   NVA - NORTH VIETNAMESE ARMY   CHINOOK- A LARGE CARGO HELICOPTER

THE
BATTLE
OF
AN NINH

In Vietnam, to save the day,
U.S. Paratroopers, went into harm's way ....
One day, in September, of sixty five,
Two deadly enemies, about to collide ....

A beautiful morn, we did greet,
No sign of the enemy, we'd soon meet ....
Hot chow, a very special treat,
So many troopers, be there time to eat .... ?

No, chow line too long, so many to feed,
Enough to bring, any enemy, to their knees ....
A swarm of helicopters, then arrived,
Rapid deployment, guarantees surprise ....

So many soldiers, have to fly by shifts,
On the third lift, assigned my niche ....
After landing, "a walk in the sun,"
A thorough search, we'd soon be done ....

The first landing went unopposed,
Back they flew, for another load ....
As they reached the LZ, not far away,
All hell broke loose, that fateful day ....

We could observe the battle flare,
As they flew into the VC snare .....
Command radios, their volume high,
Hearing the cries, of those, about to die ....

Observing choppers fall from the sky,
"More men and ammo, or all would die"......
They reported, "VC lying on their backs,
AK's roaring, in full attack"....!

As crippled choppers, flew our way,
At the chalk lines, we did pray ....
Riddled by bullets, they limped in,
Dead door gunners, our looks, chagrin .....

Off we flew, not knowing our fate,
Hoping our arrival, be not too late .....
The LZ, much too hot to land,
A hail of fire, stifling our plan .....

All our choppers, now, unfit to fly,
Must reach the airhead, before all died ....
Our artillery, bogged down, out of range,
From our brothers, we felt estranged ....

Fighter jets were then unleashed,
High explosives and Napalm,
to close the breech...
Helicopters, on loan, we obtained,
An alternate LZ, forced, we attained .....

At the airhead, our soldiers fought like hell,
Attack, after attack, they repelled ......
The battle raging, both day and night,
Charlie losing, much of his might ....

Hurt so badly, many VC ran away,
Escape and evasion, they'd fight, another day ....
As we approached, many caught in our net,
An avenging force, they had met ....

Reaching the air head, with much relief,
Heroic soldiers, we did greet ...
They devastated the enemy, in their nest,
Completely surrounded, they passed the test ....

The enemy fired on our medevacs,
Expert riflemen silenced these attacks .....
Their battlefield, we then acquired,
From a baptism of blood, our wounded retired
.....

Badly outnumbered, these troopers,
held their own,
An enemy battalion had possessed ,
that landing zone...
On that LZ, The enemy rehearsed,
To transform each helicopter, into a hearse .....

Most of our officers became casualties,
Assumption of command, not a disability ....
Sergeants led them, in their plight,
Turning defeat to victory, overnight .....

For two days, we policed that battlefield,
So much carnage and death, it was surreal ....
Fighting snipers, all that remained,
Most of that battalion, left dead or lame ....

I counted the enemy dead, in awe,
Hardly believing, just what I saw ....
Flying into the jaws of death,
These paratroopers, proven, among the best ....

To the gallant troopers of that LZ,
We salute you and your victory ......
Never has so few, fought like so many,
You crippled a battalion of the enemy .....

Looking back, it's plain to see,
Bravery is your legacy ....
The Battle of An Ninh, your victory,
Your glorious, "Rendezvous With Destiny"....

"DADDY LOVE"

photo from 101st Assoc. "Vietnam Odyssey"

Permit me, to tell the story,
The life of a humble man....
A soldier who sought no glory,
A paratrooper, named, Ben Cai Lam....
    From the communists of China,
    His family and he, did flee....
    To Saigon, "The Paris of the Orient,"
    In French Indochina, they'd be free....
They could worship,
their God of choice,
In this land, They'd have
some voice....
Here, they could own
some property,
Here, they'd raise their
family......
    But the French, did
    rule this land,
    They were fighting,
    Viet Minh, guerrilla
    bands....
    Oppressed people,
    joined the fight,
    Swelled to an army, of
    awesome might....
Ho Chi Minh, their
leader and general,
Facing him, the French did tremble....
In many battles, the French lost face,
Dien Bien Phu, their fine disgrace....
    A great house, Father Lam, had bought,
    Their home and happiness, was not lost....
    Three stories, a tiled roof, a heavy teak door,
    They kept it all, despite that war....
One day, the communists came,
To take the freedoms, they had gained....
Like locusts, they swarmed the land,
Here, the family of Lam, would take a stand...
    Nguyen Lena, the love of Ben's life,
    Beautiful Lena, someday, to be his wife...
    With tears of sadness, they had to part,
    America's longest war, was about to start....

Ben joined the Army of South Viet Nam,
To the U.S. 101st Airborne, he'd lend a hand....
As interpreter, he taught us much,
With his guidance, nothing, left to luck....

Ben's first year, with the one o' one,
He gained the friendship, of everyone...
A gallant warrior and gentleman,
He won the respect of
Lt. Col. Emerson....
"Gunfighter" Emerson,
our commanding
officer,
Would give our enemy,
absolutely, no quarter....
To the soldiers of his
"Strike Force,"
His affection is still in
order.....

Ben fought the first
year, by our side,
For us, and his country,
willing to die....
After Dak To, many
returned to the states,
Ben stayed with the 101, sharing their fate....

Ben, a "Screaming Eagle," for six years,
In all battles, he showed no fear...
The Ashau Valley, Hamburger Hill, Cambodia, Tet of 68,
A combat soldier, absolutely, first rate.....

When the 101st, left for home,
Battling cross Nam, Ben still roamed....
After Vietnamization, Ben still fought,
He would not accept, the war was lost....

An officer in the ARVN, he became,
The rank of Captain, he did obtain....
Commanding a company, he fought gallantly,
His only desire, complete victory...!

The Viet Cong swarmed South Viet Nam,
The Government of Saigon, fled in alarm....
Utter chaos, filled every street,
Province after province, fell in defeat....
Viet Cong flags, flew everywhere,
Ben left alone, in utter despair...
Disappear he must, into thin air,
A panicked population, quivered in fear....
    No place to go, caught in their web,
    Facing his captors, the spiders he dread....
    Being a leader, to prison he went,
    Chained, his back, twisted and bent. ...
Hungry, thirsty, mistreated every day,
Hard labor, his strength, melted away...
Five years, he spent in captivity,
Then his parents, bribed his way free.....
    Into the underground,
    he disappeared,
    Recapture was, his constant fear....
    Escape to America,
    became his dream,
    Silent anguish,
    his muffled scream....
To escape, he became a sailor,
Seventeen attempts, ended in failure.
Weather, Betrayal, communist scams,
All conspired to foil his plans....
    Finally, he captained a boat,
    One hundred refugees,
    would it stay afloat?
    Evading enemies, then the pirates,
    To Malaysia, cautious and quiet....
They spotted land, let out a cheer,
Ben had steered them,
free and clear...
Detained in a refugee camp,
Close quarters, dank, and cramped....
    To the U.S., Ben wrote all he knew,
    "Gunfighter", alone, stood fast and true...
    Sponsoring Ben, away he flew,
    To the land, of red, white, and blue...!
"Gunfighter's" support, gave him a home,
Off to college, he secured a loan....
Ben studied hard, earned his degree,
The General landed him a good job,
Ben moved to D.C. ...
    Ben worked hard, saved his money,
    Longed for his wife, Lena his honey....
    Finally, she boarded, that freedom plane,
    The love of his life, he had regained...!

Now Ben and Lena, have a daughter of four,
Taylor Jacqueline Lam, they so adore....
Memorial Day, Ben, brought me to his door,
My wife and I, excited to our very core...!
    We watched in awe, his love, that flows,
    Ben possesses, an inner glow....
    God and "Gunfighter", stayed by his side,
    What an honor, to see him thrive.....
Ben lets me call his daughter, "Jackie",
In honor of my brother, killed in action....
Now I have that inner glow, what a reaction...!
I've restored a friendship, everlasting....!
    I've watched him shop, "The Land of Plenty",
    He still has to watch, all his pennies....
    Every purchase, you see his joy ,
    How little "Jackie", loves her toys....

If his little one is in distress,
Ben is at his very best.....
"Don't cry", "Daddy Love, Daddy Love",
She is his blessing, from Heaven above...

I've had the honor, held her in my arms,
I have fell, under her charms....
What a lovely, little creature,
She has her parents, lovely features.....

To see them free, enjoying life,
Not dwelling on, their trouble or strife...
Makes me feel, so happy inside,
Some efforts in Viet Nam, have survived...!

To all, he owes, only one man,
    Through him, they live in,
"The Promised Land"....
Lt. Gen. Henry E. Emerson is the one,
Through him, their life, has just begun....

Now they enjoy, their beautiful home,
No longer, do they, have to roam....
They have their freedoms, share their love,
Finally obtaining, that allusive, peaceful dove...

The sweetest words, to greet my ears,
They'll stay with me, throughout my years.....
"Daddy Love, Daddy Love", oh so right,
Ben finally home, tis the end of his fight...!!!!!

"AN EAGLE HAS LANDED !"
WELCOME HOME, BEN & LENA

BUT STILL....

The odds against the combat soldier,
Are sure to set his bones, to moulder ....
BUT STILL, his courageous heart,
Drives his will, beyond what some, consider smart....

His struggles are of constant agony,
The elements, mostly, add to misery ....
Extreme heat, bitter cold, monsoon rains,
Raging waters, desert sands, jungled lands...

BUT STILL, the soldier's love of country,
So much more, than one could ask for........
Keep him faithful, to his task,
Despite the odds, he stands true and fast....

No matter the mission, what ever his condition,
He will take, that extra step....
He'll not pause, to catch his breath,
There's no time, for him to rest ....

Blinding snow, inclement weather,
Frostbit feet, freezing sleet ....
Foul weather gear, not up to par,
The enemy knows, you'll not get far....

Sleep deprivation, hunger, thirst,
The average person, would swear and curse.........
BUT STILL , the combat soldier truly knows,
His determination, will surely grow ....

The enemy plots his downfall,
A sneak attack, the bugle calls....
Using any means, to effect his kill,
To stop your heart, your blood, he'll spill....

THIS POEM WAS INSPIRED BY
THE DEDICATION AND DEATH
OF A VERY BRAVE SOLDIER...
HIS NAME WAS
SGT. RICHARD C. YOUNGBEAR .

AGE 26, HE WAS OF AMERICAN INDIAN
HERITAGE. HE WAS A MEMBER OF
CO. A, 2/502 INFANTRY, 101st AIRBORNE
DIVISION. HE WAS KILLED
IN ACTION, BY ENEMY MACHINEGUN FIRE,
AT TUY HOA, SOUTH VIET NAM
ON 03 FEBRUARY 1966.
HE WAS AWARDED THE SILVER STAR,
POSTHUMOUSLY, FOR
HIS HEROIC ACTIONS.

The unseen enemy is a threat,
He'll try to catch you, in his net....
To ambush, snipe you, use booby traps,
Any means, your pain will last ....

When the enemy is not nearby,
Unseen dangers, crawl and fly ....
Vicious animals , poisonous snakes,
Malaria, Dengue, deadly fevers, are your fate....

BUT STILL, the combat soldier will not quit,
He'll fight like hell, use his wit.....
Field expediency, put to use,
Out of nothing, he'll make soup....

Endurance, stamina, training,
Enemy ground, he'll be gaining....
Fighting for all he's worth,
Enemy soldiers, curse his birth....

Missing home, the loved ones there,
That pretty girl, prompts a tear....
Whatever obstacles, be in his path,
They'll not stop him, his love stands fast....

Suffering becomes a way of life,
Civilians can't imagine the pain, the strife......
Comfort is a thing of the past,
Fear is the enemy, you must surpass....

Survival, the only thing that matters,
Mass explosions, the blood does splatter...
To see your buddy, shot, quite dead,
His body torn, no time to mourn....

He knew the odds, his grave, so near,
He was only young, if you count his years....
He wouldn't give in, to his fears,
You must be tough, can't shed your tears....

Push on, young soldier,
Take the hill....
Death, surely, a bitter pill,
You must succeed, fire at will....

Enemy soldiers, all around you,
Buddies dying, HELL SURROUNDS YOU.. . . .
BUT STILL, you know, in your heart,
Your flag still flying, come the morning...!

Bullets pierce your tender flesh,
BUT STILL you fight, with your last breath. . . !
VICTORY, you take the hill,
Your spirit soars, only your heart,
is BUT STILL....!

Dedicated to our gallant service people who made the supreme sacrifice.
Their bravery and dedication will never be forgotten.
Rest in peace, your Flag still flies, your grateful country, still survives.
VETERAN'S DAY, NOVEMBER 11, 1995.

DOGS CANNOT GO TO HEAVEN

Dogs - God's gift to mankind - true friends, brave soldiers and natural PTSD specialist...

DOGS CAN NOT GO TO HEAVEN, so some people say,
Perhaps, only because,
they give us some of it each day...
I purchased Nikki, when just a pup,
Now remembering, how he cheered me up...

A tiny Chocolate Labrador, who scampered and played,
Czar Nicholas, "Nikki," brightened every day...
Always a true and loyal friend,
For twelve years, as a member of our family,
he did blend...

With my son, Brent, he loved to play,
Retrieving tennis balls, Brent threw far away...
Taking him swimming we had great fun,
With Zack, our yellow Lab, how they would run...

Leaping into the water with a great bound,
Splashing all who were around ... !
A contest, you see, who would be first to get the stick,
So much fun performing these tricks...

Nikki was the stronger of the two,
But buddies, they were bound like glue...
Dominance settled, Nikki would reign,
But Zack would challenge, in every game...

A test of strength and endurance, went on each day,
Jealous of each other, they'd growl, then play...
Never would they hurt one another,
Slowly, they became each other's brother...

Come feeding time, at each other, they would bark,
Balanced portions were no lark ...
How Nikki loved to eat,
Wolfing it down, Zack to beat ...

Everyday, when I came home,
Nice to know, my family, never left alone...
Our person, home and property, they would protect,
This great responsibility, they'd not neglect ... !

Nikki, always wanting to please,
Learning new tricks with great ease...
Perhaps beating Zack, his secret inspiration,
But a dog biscuit treat, still brought elation...

How he loved to ride in the back of my truck,
Knowing he was in the luck...
Going somewhere, a special treat,
He liked this much more, than "time to eat"...!

Whenever I got feeling down,
Playing with Nikki, I'd loose that frown...
Such a beautiful animal,
giving so much devotion and affection,
Chasing away the blues, he offered much protection ... !

But on Nikki time took its toll,
His last year he looked so tired and old...
But still he'd insist on playing,
Didn't matter, his chocolate coat rapidly greying...

His last couple days, he was really sick,
But still to please, his last wish...
So sick he could barely raise his head,
Zack finally winning, "time to be fed"...

Dogs are smarter than some people say,
Zack knew Nikki passed away...
Unusually quiet and somber he watched me work,
As I covered his brother, with God's good earth...

I think there were tears in his eyes, the same as mine,
Both feeling so sorry, our buddy, Nikki, ran out of time...
DOGS CAN NOT GO TO HEAVEN, so some people say,
But to see Nikki and me there, I'll continue to pray...
        for I know, he'd brighten my stay....!

THEY STILL BECKON TO ME...!

As darkness fell, we entered an eerie hell,
The dead and dying were all over the place...
Grotesque looks frozen on every face,
Alive or dead- from here, there was no escape...

Fighting our way into this hell,
Dead bodies were already beginning to swell ....
The smell of sulfur and cordite filled the air,
This bamboo jungle reeked an ominous fear....

Amidst the moans and cries for help,
You imagined the banshees shriek and yelp....
A mist settled in, shrouding
the ground with a ghostly air,
You were in their forbidden, demonic lair....

Enemy soldiers were heard creeping about,
A glimpse of khaki prompted fire and shouts....
Charlie, nearly invisible, as he sniped at us,
As soldiers fell, he reveled in his lust....

We formed a perimeter in two-man teams,
Piercing eyes strained to see what they could glean....
Fifteen minutes only, one watch could serve,
Vision purple must be preserved...

As the night slowly settled in,
Goose pimples and hair stood on skin....
Quiet. Listen. Did you hear that?,
Like snakes, the enemy crawled on bellies flat....

Just behind, where I lay prone,
A row of dead soldiers had slowly grown....
Six corpses, in camouflaged tiger fatigues,
lay on their backs,
They had died in their fierce, savage attack....

My partner, then I, would lay in wait,
Carefully watching to kill all snakes....
First his turn, then again, it would be mine,
Noticing the corpses had moved each time ... !

Rigor-mortis was creating a morbid display,
Arms and legs would slowly sway....
In the hot, muggy climate decomposition was very fast,
Creating images - forever to last....

All night long, the dead seemed to beckon me,
Their arms slowly signaling, come-
join me in eternity...!
Sporadic fire lasted all night long,
The wounded moaning their sorrowful song....

Chainsaws worked to clear a landing zone,
Combat engineers dodging bullets amidst the groans....
The jungle too thick for a chopper to land,
Baskets filled by bloody hands....

The choppers' flood light illuminated ghostly figures,
As enemy snipers, tightened fingers
round their triggers....
Muzzle flashes were answered by hails of fire,
Angry soldiers stifling a situation most dire....

Throughout the long and surreal night,
The extraction of the wounded and dead took flight....
By dawn the worst had passed,
But the scenes of that night would forever last....

Now, many years have come and gone,
But the images of that night still linger on....
In my troubled sleep, I can clearly see,
Those dead soldiers, waving,
THEY STILL BECKON TO ME...

"When one goes to war, one never returns home the same; albeit, forever changed."

- Peter S. Griffin

TEARS

John Thomas Griffin

Oswego, NY
Born January 5, 1927

U.S. Army
Corporal
Serial Number 12297322

Killed in Action
March 25, 1951

*Corporal Griffin was a member of Company G, 2nd Battalion,
187th Airborne Infantry Regimental Combat Team. He was
dropped behind enemy lines near Musan-ni, South Korea on
March 23, 1951 as a part of an airborne assault to block
20,000 Chinese troops. His mission was accomplished but he
was Killed in Action during the fighting on March 25, 1951.
Corporal Griffin was awarded the Good Conduct Medal, the
Purple Heart, the Combat Infantry Badge, the Presidential
Unit Citation, the Korean Service Medal, the UN Service
Medal, the Korean Presidential Unit Citation and the
Parachute Insignia.*

THE KOREAN WAR VETERANS HONOR ROLL

A SOLDIER IS NO MORE

Death, my friend, comes to everyone,
If one is old, it is not so shunned...
But to lose one's life, before it's begun,
Is a loss, that leaves all stunned...

For a young man to go to war,
To love his country, enough to die for....
Is a noble thing indeed,
To give up all, for his friends in need....

Politics do not play a part,
A soldier's love is from the heart....
To toil and suffer all day long,
To give his all, to right a wrong....

To ease the suffering of those in need,
Is, my friend, a noble deed....
For he was hungry, cold, and wet,
But still he fought, and his eyes wept....

For you see, before death came,
He laid his eyes upon the lame...
He saw the evil that men can do,
He saw the hatred, as it grew....

War is hell upon our earth,
A curse we fight, from its birth....
For when men can't get along,
Battle lines are often drawn....

When "A soldier is no more",
Death was caused by an act of war....
He suffered much, in his pain,
He gave his life, for our gain....

We owe him a debt that we can't pay
He sacrificed all his days....
He lost his love, and child dear,
So we could live, without the fear....

We are obliged to carry on,
He would want us to be strong....
For us to live our whole life free,
We turn his death - to victory....

"A soldier is no more", or less,
Than our country's very best....
For one to martyr his own life,
The ultimate sacrifice, for our plight....

He gave his life for you and me,
Never forget, it was willingly....
For my friend, his death will never be,
Just a fading memory....

They say, "Old Soldiers Just Fade Away,"
That's not true, they risked their days....
There is no better thing to do,
To serve your flag, your whole life through...

A soldiers life is always condensed,
A life of service, to be spent....
They know when they take up arms,
To love and serve, in spite of harm...

"A soldier is no more" than this,
The winds most silent, loving kiss....
The bright sun, lighting all our days,
The tears shed, upon his grave....

Rest in peace, my brother gone,
I'll think of you, not forlorn....
For I know your spirit soars,
Tis heaven's gain, "A soldier is no more"....

Dedicated to the author's brother CPL John T. Griffin -
Co. G, 2 / 187th ARCT-KIA, Korea- 25 March,1951

"ONE OF THE BOYS"

One of the Boys have left our ranks,
One of the troopers, who covered our flanks . . .
A soldier true, through and through,
One who loved, the red white and blue....

He loved America with all his heart,
He loved his buddies, never to part. . .
His time has come, we will miss him so,
Hearts are broken, spirits are low....

He answered the call, he gave his all,
He saw us through, he paid his dues . . .
A true friend, rarer than a unicorn,
A soldier who, weathered the storms . . .

He was there, for all of us,
He fought the battles fair and just....
By our side, our friend and guide,
The gates of heaven, are open wide....

Battle after battle, he fought his way,
Side by side, he kept the stride .....
Fighting hard, to turn the tide,
Spreading freedom far and wide....

He was with us, "One of the Boys",
When the going got tough, he had the right stuff...
A soldier, on which you could always depend,
A warrior, a brother, and a true friend ....

He never wore a frown, he never let us down,
Encouraging us all, always walking tall....
Proud, he was, and rightfully so,
Paving the way, he was always on the go.....

After the war, he was never far away,
He was always there, to brighten all our days...
Few men have ever given quite as much as he,
Serving God and country in quiet dignity ....

It is very hard to stand here,
Fighting back the tears.....
My mind is really racing,
Remembering all the years...

Percy M. Gibson Jr. (Brenda
Griffin's father) is shown receiving the
Bronze Star - Salzburg, Austria 1944
"One of the Boys"

Quite hard my friends to put into words,
To salute a great soldier, a friend such as he...
His love will last eternally,
His spirit will always be with me....

I will never forget, what he meant to me,
His friendship can't be kept in a diary.....
Perhaps it is, enough to say,
"One of the Boys" still leads the way.....

OUR CHILD, TORN AND TATTERED

A gift of love, from Heaven above,
Blessed we are, God's consecration of love....
A baby born, to share our life,
A bundle of joy, to protect day and night....
    A mother's joy, a father's pride,
    Her laughter, makes our smiles wide....
    Her first step, a gigantic stride,
    Our hearts are open, far and wide....
To come home, after a hard day's work,
To see her smile, makes it all worthwhile....
To play with her and make her laugh,
Will warm, winter's coldest draft....
    A baby makes a house a home,
    A restless heart, will cease to roam....
    A husband's and wife's love, thus bonded,
    Forms a weld, that can't be parted....
To see her grow, to guide her so,
To watch her blossom, and flower....
To become a young lady, right and proper,
To see your guidance, shine and prosper....
    You thank God, all day long,
    For making such a miracle, all your own....
    Her first tears, break your heart,
    Her first kiss, her feelings start....
To see her knowledge, grow and leap,
Her compassion, full and sweet....
To see such innocence, white as snow,
Off to college, she must go....
    Preparations will take all summer,
    New friends, she'll soon discover....
    Making friends and forming relations,
    Fills her heart with anticipation....
Gone with friends, to see a movie,
Full of life, music, oh so groovy....
Then it happens, in a flash,
A dreaded phone call, there's been a crash....
    "She's seriously injured," they're quick to relate,
    "It appears brain damage, is her fate"....
    Many attempts, but no response,
    "I'm afraid her prognosis....,
    there's much to want"....

"Please dear God, don't let it be
"If you must, please take me...!"
"She's so young, don't let her go,
"Let her live, we love her so...!"
    Many dark days were to follow,
    Our hearts broken and spirits hallow.....
    Praying to God, for courage and strength,
    Our faith in Him, would not relent.....
As time passed, God healed her wounds,
Doctors encouraged, her strength resumed....
Many obstacles to overcome,
From love of God, her determination sprung....
    Working hard, she fought back tears,
    Family and friends, allayed her fears...
    Mom and Dad, praying day and night,
    God gave them all, the will to fight....
Little brother, a brave ally,
Always staying, by her side.....
Sharing a room, to fight the gloom,
He made her laugh, he fed her by spoon....
    Always showing her confidence,
    His love and concern, filled the room....
    Helping her, with physical therapy,
    His brotherly love, a bright, shining clarity....
After several operations,
And many months of recuperation.....
We were filled with divine elation,
Life was filled, with new inspiration.....
    To have "Our child torn and tattered,"
    Our family life was really rattled.....
    But by keeping, God's good faith,
    He restored us, to his saving grace.....
Now she's grown, very well educated,
A loving husband, her friend and guide.....
Two little girls, God's creations,
The noble healing profession, is her vocation....
    We wish you joy, health, happiness, and long life,
    For you have conquered, many a strife....
    Now, as you watch your family, prosper and grow,
    Always remember, we love you so.....

Dad, Mom, Brent and Family... God Bless you, Pam

As a small boy I had the privilege to observe,
True love blossom and emerge....
My beautiful sister, Gail, so young and petite,
Full of life, true and sweet....

Raised a few blocks from our street,
A handsome lad, she did meet....
His name was Teddy, who was several years older,
"Don't talk to him", our Mother did scold her ... !

Teddy was a soldier, you see,
Mother leery of what his intentions might be....
But Gail had caught Teddy's eye,
He fell deeply 'in love', of that, he wouldn't deny....

Mother granted absolutely no quarter,
So very cautiously, he tried to court her....
Gail was smitten by Teddy's charm and affection,
Caught dating him she earned detention....

FOR HER TEDDY

Not wanting to provoke more of Mothers' wrath,
Teddy decided to try a different tact....
He assured our parents, a gentleman, he'd surely be,
If they could only, date occasionally....

Granted permission, they shared great times,
Once Mom got to know Teddy, all was fine....
Still leery of Mom, for over six months, Gail never got a kiss,
She had to beg and plead for Teddy to grant that wish ... !

When visiting us, he gave me gifts,
Military patches, "K" and "C" rations, he granted my wish....
Making camp with my little friends,
Many campfire meals cooked at that rivers' bend....

For me, Teddy became another big brother,
A soldier friend like no other....
He made me feel like I was all grown up,
Drinking hot coffee from a canteen cup...

After nine years service, he earned final his discharge,
France, Germany, Iceland, he had seen the world at large....
Now his only desire was family life,
Fulfilling his dream, Gail became his loving wife...

Teddy and Gail remodeled a house, made it their home,
Their love and happiness radiantly shown....
Sharing a love so pure and true,
Their darling children numbered two....

How they cherished the lives they made,
Stephanie and Rick, such joy, they gave....
Teddy loved to watch them learn and play,
His family brightened all his days....

Teddy worked hard and provided well,
Many a humorous story he was known to tell....
Always a smile and pleasant greeting,
He offered all, upon their meeting....

Of all things, Teddy loved his family and our country's flag,
A dedicated patriot, he'd carry this love all his days....
He loved a cold beer, with veterans near,
At the American Legion Hall, he held so dear....

After a days work he loved to lay on his personal divan,
John Wayne and vintage war movies completed his plan....
Many an hour he enjoyed, passing that way,
Home, hearth, wife, their children safe at play....

As Teddy grew older, his heart grew weak,
Bypass surgery required or his future bleak....
With silent prayers, his family by his side,
A successful outcome, a merciful God let him survive....

Stephanie grew into a beautiful young lass and married well,
Grandchildren, Jackie and Allison, just lovely, I'm proud to tell...
A father and son team, Rick became Teddy's best friend,
On boating and fishing trips, their affections did blend....

God surely did bless this family with many graces,
Well mannered boys and pretty girls with fancy laces....
Gail always kept an immaculate home,
Polished floors, brass, silver and chrome....

That successful surgery bought Teddy twelve more years,
But it could not allay all Gail's or family fears...
As time went by there were complications,
Teddy faced each new day with love, cheer and anticipation....

He was thankful and made good the time it bought,
He fought bravely but eventually his battle was lost...
Teddy taught us all the love of family life,
To cherish each other and do what's right....

Atop his grave is the flag he loved so dear,
It gently waves in the clean, brisk, fresh air....
Gail knows in Heaven, a celestial couch was made ready,
God prepared it special, for the love of her life, just FOR HER TEDDY...

IN LOVING MEMORY OF
the Author's brother-in-law,
FREDERICK E. JONES

My Sister, dear...

for Lynn Griffin LaRock

There is a part of my heart,
No one can own....
It belongs to my sister,
My sister alone....
Blessed by God, in Heaven above,
Bestowed on me, this blessing of love...
My darling girl, my sister, fair,
My friend, my companion, held so dear...
To grace my life, God's gift to me,
A sister, to share life, in perfect harmony....
To grow together, all through life,
To weather the storms and darkest nights....
As lyrics and music, blend to song,
Sister and brother, so belong....
Brought together, by God above,
Belong together, as hand and glove....
Hand in hand, through life we traveled,
Tightening a bond, never to unravel....
Sharing our happiness and our tears,
Our love sustained us, through the years....
Sharing together, hearth and home,
Special times and smiles renown....
To watch our families, as they grew,
Raising children, sweet and true....

How I love you, MY SISTER, DEAR,
For all you've given, all your years....
For your husband, your children, grand babies new,
How they look and act, just like you....
Thank you, so much, MY SISTER, DEAR,
For loving us, throughout the years....
You brightened our days, allayed our fears,
Your smiling face, always so near....
You taught us, what courage really is,
To rely on Jesus, His powers within....
To count our blessings and give thanks, above,
To obtain forever, God's lasting love....
Now God has called you, to his home,
Welcomed, you stand, before his throne....
Thank him, please, MY SISTER, DEAR,
For the love He's given, all your years....
Rest in peace, my sister, gone,
A part of my heart, to you belongs....
Take it with you, as you go,
Pray to God, your footsteps, I'll follow....

In loving memory of MY SISTER, DEAR....

EIGHTEEN
IN THE MORROW

A mother writes her cherished son,
Away in Korea, a war to be won....
Keeping the home fires, warm and burning,
In her heart, her oldest baby, she is yearning....

    Little brother, peeks in the door,
    He see's the worry, she does store....
    Too young to know, the horrors of war,
    But upset, about the tears that poured....

"Tell him, I'll be EIGHTEEN IN THE MORROW,"
Old enough, to end her sorrow....?
A startled look, upon her face,
She prays to God, for saving grace....

    "Enclosing a medal, and a prayer,
    To keep you safe, while you are there....
    I'll write you faithfully, every day,
    I'll pray for you, while you're away....

"Wear the medal, while we're apart,
Wear it just, above your heart....
Our loving God, will keep you safe,
Till you're home, to resume your place"....

    It is March 7th, of fifty-one,
    Been a year, since the war begun,
    Winter winds, the snows are blowing,
    A sad premonition, she is knowing....

She harbours the fear, death, so near,
Oh, so hard, to hide the tears....
"Tell him, Mom, I'll soon be there,"
As he climbs, up on her chair....

    Little brother, holds her near,
    Too small to comfort, her growing fears....
    "Don't worry, Mother, I'll keep him safe,"
    To ease the worry, on her face....

"I'll be EIGHTEEN IN THE MORROW,"
Forget the years, that he'll borrow.
In her heart, a glimmer shines,
Innocence is so sublime....

    "Don't worry, Jack, help is coming,
    Pete's joining the paratroops, in the morning....
    Says, he'll help fight, that old war,
    "We dare not tell him, he's just four...."

Corporal John T. Griffin never received the letter, it was returned marked "DECEASED".
He was killed in action, 25 March 51, Co G, 2/187 ARCT, at Parun-ni, South Korea.
Pete was "EIGHTEEN IN THE MORROW", like so many others, fighting the war in Viet Nam.

Dancing With Terry

Terry in high school

Dorthea, my sister, what a lovely gal,
So many qualities, but most of all, my pal....
A large family, children, numbered ten,
When Mom was busy, Dorthea, became my "Mother Hen"...

Her little brother, she made me behave,
Always so gentle, not a hand on me, was laid....
Big brother, Terry, correcting every move,
Always so worried, wanting none of us, to lose....

He was prim and proper, but he could agitate,
He had all the answers, us siblings, he would educate....
Dorthea, so self conscience, her feelings, she would show,
Terry knew her weakness, of crying, he'd make her go....

Not much changed, as the years went by,
Terry and Dorthea, attending Catholic High....
Terry being bossy, Dorthea, cute and shy,
At every opportunity, he'd always make her cry....

How Dorthea loved to dance,
With her sisters, she would prance....
Music filled her very soul,
Terry studying, would always shout and scold...!

To Terry, being smart, the way to impress,
To Dorthea, being pretty, and how she dressed...
Terry's friends, so important, they had class,
Dorthea, just wanting, all the fun to last....

A gala dance, scheduled at Catholic High,
"Don't you jitterbug and shake your thighs...!
If you embarrass me, in front of my friends,
your dancing days will come to an end...!"

Dorthea, so proud, and looking so fine,
Left the house crying, like she committed a crime...!
She was so beautiful, in her new dress,
She stood out, way, above the rest....

Terry's friends swarmed her, asking to dance,
One by one, they fell under her trance....
Terry, shyly asked, "Will you dance with me?"
Dorthea STRONGLY refused, relishing in her victory...!

Many years passed, but they remembered that night,
They shared a lesson, taught, ever so right...
Each person, became their own,
In love and respect, they had grown....

Both fulfilled their lot in life,
Early death, by cancer, became their plight...
Both raised families, beautiful and strong,
Now part of their life, I'm proud to belong....

Love your family, they taught us all,
Life is fleeting, make it a gala ball...!
Let's share love of life, and all be merry,
For we'll soon see, Dorthea, DANCING WITH TERRY...!!

Dorthea in high school

I love and miss you guys, your little brother, - Pete.

A MOTHER'S APRON STRINGS

Dedicated to my mother,
Leita E. Griffin ,
in honor and respect
for all our Gold Star Mothers,
all veterans hearts are joined with theirs.

The bond between a mother and her son,
Is a love that can never he undone....
It starts before infancy, last infinitely,
Endures all hardships, a lasting partnership....

To see him grow each step of the way,
Knowing he'll be a fine man, someday....
To comfort him when he's ill,
To bandage the scrapes, from his spills....

To wipe away his tears,
Your apron strings will guide him,
through the years...
To watch his excitement at discovery,
To love and nurse him, through recovery....

To see his Face, break into a smile,
To watch him grow, through every mile...
His first kiss makes him tingle,
His relationships grow, as he mingles....

Puppy loves cause broken hearts,
It's so hard, when young love parts.....
To see his knowledge leap and grow,
To right small wrongs, he does sow.....

To see him graduate and become a man,
To become a patriot, to protect our land ....
To go off to fight, for what is right,
To pray for him, those days and nights...

To receive the word, that he's been killed,
In a far away land, his blood's been spilled....
He gave his life for God and man,
You can't accept the loss, it's not your plan.....!

They give to you, a Mother's Gold Star,
Can your apron strings reach that far...?
Your heart is broken beyond repair,
If only you could hold him, oh so near .....

Precious memories are all that's left,
Faded photographs, child's toys, that you kept...
Cherished letters, you saved from him,
To live life without him, where to begin....?

Draped over that old kitchen chair,
Your apron, the strings that held him near...
Put it around you, tie it tight,
His loving arms, will comfort your plight....

Now, mother's gone, with apron white,
To that star, that shines so bright...
To us, she leaves, a gift so right,
A MOTHER'S APRON STRINGS,
TO GUIDE US THOUGH OUR DARKEST NIGHTS....

In loving memory of our mother, Leita,
All her children

Photo: *"Airborne Mom"* - Leita Griffin

IN HONOR OF ...

IN HONOR OF.... those troopers we lost,
IN HONOR OF.... those who, bore the cost....
Liberty, for all, is what they sought,
America's freedom, the gift, they bought....

IN HONOR OF.... those who shouted, "FOLLOW ME!",
Their sacred path... to victory....
IN HONOR OF.... Rudy, George, Chuck and Dave,
All those, who sacrificed, all their days...

Fallen Screaming Eagles, brothers... so true,
They preserved, the Red, White and Blue....
IN HONOR OF.... the lives they gave,
IN HONOR OF.... all... all their names....

IN MEMORY OF _____

In memory of _____, and the other great guys,
Who fought the war, by my side.....
Enduring all, that came his way,
_____laid down his life, that fateful day...

Battle after battle, he led the way,
From his duty, refused to sway....
Soaring with Eagles, Airborne All the Way,
Only God, family and me.., to preserve his memory.....

FOR MOTHERS AND PARATROOPERS

Thinking back, across the years,
Many remembrances bring forth the tears....
My earliest recollection of those days gone by,
Just a little boy, Mother, drying tears from my eyes....

Standing by a flag draped coffin,
Bewildered by what was in the offing....
Two uniformed soldiers stood at attention,
A priest offering words of comfort and affection .....

Family and friends paying their last respects,
As my parents gasped for breath....
In that closed coffin lay their first born,
My paratrooper brother, who I so adored .....

I was just a lad of four,
From my eyes, the tears just poured,
For you see, he was a hero to me,
Now he was gone, replaced, by unwanted sympathy....

I remember, looking, way up at him,
How he'd smile and flash that grin....
He'd pick me up, set me on his knee,
Showing the love, he had for me....

He'd tell me stories, that were so brave,
Jumping from airplanes, he wasn't afraid .....
Told me, when I was bigger, I could do it too,
Wouldn't be long, I could serve the
Red, White and Blue .....

Said he had to go to Korea, to fight in a war,
Flipped me a half dollar, for candy at the store....
"Don't worry, Pete, I'll be all right,
It's my job, I'm trained to fight"....

There was no doubt, he'd be just fine,
How his jump boots, cast that shine....
That glider patch sewed to his hat,
That Infantry braid, around his shoulder, fast....

Those silver wings upon his chest,
They only gave those, to the very best....
That blue scarf, just for guys real tough,
That "AIRBORNE" patch, the finishing touch....

Had no doubt, that he'd be fine,
Had no idea, we had so little time .....
After he left, my Mom would cry,
Didn't understand that last, goodbye .....

Now, standing there, feeling so sad and alone,
What was this coffin doing in my home ... ?
I don't believe it, he can't be dead,
This is not the way, it was supposed to end .....

Everybody's leaving, getting in their cars,
Not saying "goodbye", they can't go far....
Soon we end up at the church,
The priest says the eulogy, from his perch....

They say nice things, that I don't want to hear,
I look around around feel a growing fear....
Soon it's time, we leave again,
Will this nightmare, ever end ... ?

As we travel, I look back,
See the hearse, big, sleek and black....
As we enter the cemetery gate,
Wishing something, could change our fate....

As they lowered him into the ground,
I looked around, my heart did pound .....
Everybody, everybody, was in tears,
My Mother, holding that flag, oh so near....

"Don't cry Mother, it will be all right,"
Not knowing if it would end her plight .....
Didn't realize at that tender age,
There was no coming back, from the grave .....

When I got older, I also went to war,
Fought many battles on distant shores....
Lost many, many friends, oh so dear,
Thinking back across the years....

How many folded flags, must Mothers hold,
For gallant paratroopers, so young and bold....
It is time for all, to catch our breath,
FOR MOTHERS AND PARATROOPERS,
let's bow our heads, and reflect....

A SOLDIER'S WILL

Death has found me, on the battlefields of freedom,
Grieve not, for liberty's light shines as a beacon....
I leave to you, the things I held most dear,
Sacred, precious gifts of the highest tier....

Unto you, I bequeath, Old Glory, Lady Liberty,
The home of the brave, the land of the free....
The Bill of Rights, our Constitution,
Our halls of justice, our educational institutions....

I give to you, one nation, under God,
The many freedoms, on which, He's blessed our sod...
The right to worship, vote, love, work and play,
Not the least, of which, the things you have to say....

But most of all, I leave to you, my legacy,
For without sacrifice, there is no victory....
A SOLDIER'S WILL, preserves freedom's continuity,
A SOLDIER'S WILL, fulfills our ...

"RENDEZVOUS WITH DESTINY"

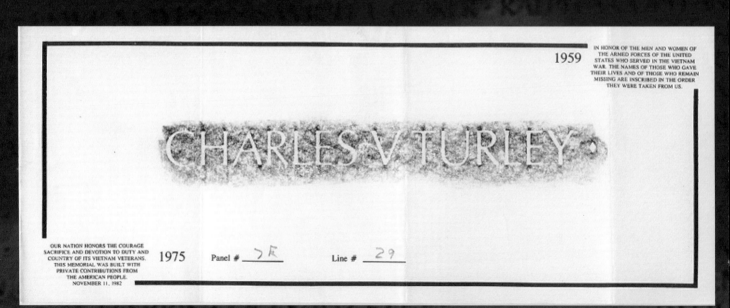

1959

IN HONOR OF THE MEN AND WOMEN OF
THE ARMED FORCES OF THE UNITED
STATES WHO SERVED IN THE VIETNAM
WAR. THE NAMES OF THOSE WHO GAVE
THEIR LIVES AND OF THOSE WHO REMAIN
MISSING ARE INSCRIBED IN THE ORDER
THEY WERE TAKEN FROM US.

CHARLES V TURLEY

OUR NATION HONORS THE COURAGE
SACRIFICE AND DEVOTION TO DUTY AND
COUNTRY OF ITS VIETNAM VETERANS.
THIS MEMORIAL WAS BUILT WITH
PRIVATE CONTRIBUTIONS FROM
THE AMERICAN PEOPLE.
NOVEMBER 11, 1982

1975   Panel # 7E   Line # 29

A SOLDIER'S PREMONITION

In Viet Nam, my friend, came up to me,
Had a strong premonition of what, was to be....
"Please take my place, on patrol, in the morning,
Or I'll surely be killed, I've had my warning"....

"There's absolutely, no doubt, in my mind,
I've never had a feeling, of this kind"....
"If I go, I'm sure to die,
About this, I would not lie"....

A look of terror, clearly, on his face,
To avoid this duty, certainly, no disgrace....
"Sure buddy, I'll prepare tonight,
If our sergeant says, it will be all right"....

Unfortunately, permission, was not to be,
To call in artillery, was unknown to me....
As a forward observer, I was not trained,
No time to learn, this was no game....

In the morning, he left, with his patrol,
His feeling of doom, followed, like his shadow....
I don't know. Certainly, he's not right,
But today, I pray, he doesn't have to fight....

Shortly, I left, with our main force,
Destiny, we'd both have to follow our course...
In the distance, a vicious firefight, I heard,
Worry, began to touch, my every nerve....

My buddy called, needed help urgently,
Fighting a large force of VC....
Through Michelin Plantation, we raced like hell,
To reach them, in time, we could not tell....

Suddenly, artillery exploded in the trees,
He mistook us, for more VC....
"Please Dear God, don't let this be,
Redlegs, Redlegs, hold your damn volleys"...!

Tragically, precious time was lost,
Dear God, what would this error cost?
As we neared, their vicinity,
The enemy disappeared, into obscurity....

Suddenly, his nightmare, came into view,
Now, no doubt, I could see it too....
My dear friend, lay dead, at my feet,
Shocked into sadness and stunned disbelief....

If only, I could have, taken his place,
My lack of knowledge, could have changed his fate....
"Ours is not to reason why, ours is but, to do and die",
A SOLDIER'S PREMONITION, will forever, make me cry....

All were killed on that patrol, that fateful day, 10 Dec. 1965

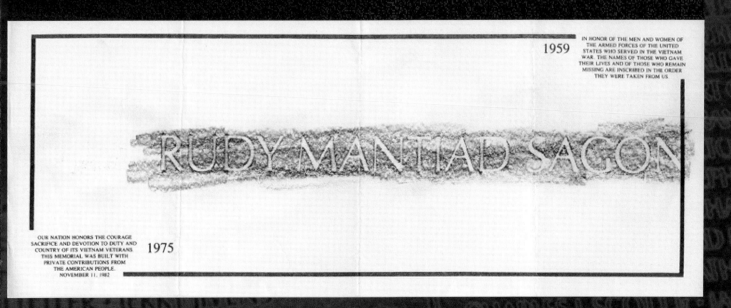

THE GHOSTS OF HILL 553

An Khe, South Viet Nam, fall, 1965,
U.S. soldiers fighting for their lives....
Highway 19 snakes through Meng Yeng Pass,
Here a French force breathed their last....

Here the Viet Cong must not be lured,
A strategic position, it must be secured....
Soon, the 1st Calvary Division, new to arrive,
Through this pass, their convoy must survive....

Hill 553 looms high above this pass,
Almost completely covered in elephant grass....
Its lofty crests must be occupied,
If taken by the enemy, many would die....

So our Infantry company, given the task
Eager to accomplish, all that was asked ....
A very steep climb, to reach its peak,
Here our guns, would have a long reach ....

Along its top we made our way,
Detecting anti-personnel mines to our dismay ....
All along its massive crest,
Three pronged monsters, hiding in their nests ....

Through the elephant grass it was hard to see,
On hands and knees, bayonets probed the earth, warily
Soon an explosion, screams of agony,
A torn and mangled Paratrooper, faced eternity...

Medics scrambling to his aid,
Into a dust off he was laid....
Bleeding profusely, one leg gone,
Soon to the Almighty, he'd belong....

Another blast, another trooper fell,
Bouncing Betty's worsened this hell....
Exploding at shoulder height,
Decapitation, quickly, snuffed out life...

One area contained a group of trees,
A Bamboo Viper brought a trooper to his knees....
Three steps was all he got,
Its venom killed, quick as a shot...

All this activity attracted snipers,
Now the Viet Cong became our vipers....
They found perches in nearby hills,
Through high powered scopes, sought out their kills....

A fifty caliber machine gun, we put into action,
Enemy snipers, soon lost their attraction....
They'd fire once, our gun would respond.
Our patrols would go out, but like ghosts,
the enemy was not found....

Snipers and mines remained a constant threat,
Unseen dangers, lurked wherever you crept....
Paths were cleared and marked with strung out paper,
A gentle wind, shifting the paper,
created a clear and present danger....

Fatigue and worry were taking its toll,
Even to defecate, you were afraid to go....
Each step could be your last,
Even mess call could turn to "Taps"...!

At dusk, one night we got the word,
An enemy assault would soon emerge....
The order given, "stay in your positions,
Sergeants don't check your men,
under any conditions"....

As darkness fell the wind began to howl,
The elephant grass rustled and seemed to scowl....
As the night dragged on, nerves were frayed,
As the grass stooped and swayed ....
the troopers prayed .....

No moon, nor stars were out that night,
Nothing to cast the slightest light....
Eerie sounds seemed to fill the air,
The winds carrying them from ear to ear....

The wail of the banshees could be heard,
As nervous fingers to triggers stirred....
In front of me, not twenty feet away,
The outline of a person, slowly crept my way...

Shouting the password, I held my fire,
Three times I challenged, my situation dire....
No response was given from the figure,
As my finger tightened around the trigger....

Stopping his advance, crouching low in the grass,
Not wearing American equipment, I saw at a glance....
An enemy soldier he must be,
that's why he won't answer me!
FIRE! FIRE! my mind told me,
survival must be my priority...

I saw his body roll down the hill,
Scared and nervous, knowing I may have killed....
Another soldier and I ran down to him,
The horror of my life, about to begin...

An American sergeant lay at our feet,
As I stared in disbelief .. !
MEDIC! MEDIC! we screamed in fear,
Oh God, dear God, please help us here...

We bandaged him as help arrived,
Covered in blood I knew he'd die....
Forming a chain of men we got him up the hill,
A helicopter whisked him away
as the night grew still....

Thanking God no one stepped on a mine,
Praying to God he would survive....
If only I could take his place,
Please Dear God, send your saving grace...

Eventually the word got back to me,
The sergeant belonged to God and eternity ....
I knew forever I had changed,
Not forgiving myself, I'd carry the blame ....

I fought many battles after Hill 553,
Their horrors and death still remain with me....
I saw many soldiers die too young,
Never have figured, just what was won....

As I look back across the years,
I still have to wipe away the tears....
Flashbacks and nightmares fill my mind,
If only I could turn back time....

I'll never know why things are meant to be,
As a mere mortal I must accept my destiny....
But with Gods help I'll seek peace and fight PTSD,
Please pray for me and THE GHOSTS OF HILL 553....

This poem is based on the true story of a good and dear friend, a dedicated soldier and a fine man, Joe Ladanyi Jr.

MY HEART WAS TOUCHED

Through tearing eyes, MY HEART WAS TOUCHED,
A dying soldier, who cares so much....
His flesh, badly torn, his heart so weak,
He's giving his life, for his beliefs....

For the girl, he left behind,
To kiss her lips, just one more time....
A lonely tear, runs down his cheek,
Her precious memory, forever, he'll keep....

He grasps my hand, as if to speak,
He can not talk, he is too weak....
MY HEART WAS TOUCHED, for I knew,
He's saying, "Good Bye", he loved me too....

My brother soldier, my friend, so true,
I swear, I'll forever, remember you....
For our country, he loved so much,
Through tearing eyes, MY HEART WAS TOUCHED....

WARRIORS OF THE BROKEN HEART

Listen America, it's time you knew,
What WARRIORS OF THE BROKEN HEART, anguish through....
In Viet Nam, they gave their all,
Won their battles at Khe Sanh, Dak to, and the Ashau....

In every campaign, they won them all,
Their battle histories, stand clear and tall....
Understanding this, how then, did Saigon fall?
The answer, not written, upon "the Wall"...!

Search your heart and mind, answer true,
Protest not, your flag, of red, white and blue....
Permit your military, to fight, with hands untied,
Zero tolerance, for weak politicians, and their lies....

In Old Glory's wars, Purple Hearts, are won,
Listen not, to protesters, as their songs be sung....
Support your soldiers, they suffer and die - FOR YOU,
WARRIORS OF THE BROKEN HEART, undeserved, their love so true....

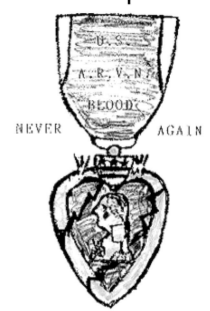

"SINCERITY IS THE DELICATE FABRIC ANGEL'S WINGS ARE MADE OF"

PLEA TO SAINT MICHAEL -
PATRON SAINT OF PARATROOPERS

Dear Saint Michael, please answer this plea,
Wrap your protective shield, all about me....
Please stop my torments, that never cease,
Evil horrors, that Satan has unleashed....

Agonies befall me, both day and night,
A battle that, I can no longer fight....
All my struggles, have been in vain,
Gone on too long, can't bear the pain....

This war has gone on... so very long,
Completely worn down, no longer strong....
My enemies attack from every side,
Finally I accept defeat and long to die....

If not in your power, to end this pain,
Ask God to admit me... to his heavenly domain....
For without you, this war is lost,
I can no longer... bear its cost....

I have but one fear, Satan will conquer me,
So Dear Saint Michael, answer this plea...
Lay me on your shield, carry me home,
If God permits, lay me at the foot of his throne....

It was an honor to fight, for God and freedom,
If only our people,
would understand the reasons....
Evil still stalks... God's blessed earth,
My dying wish, they come to appreciate,
the warriors worth...!

Please pray for peace, your combat veterans, and the defeat of PTSD.

JUST SOLDIERS

These men, who went off to war,
Came home to face, society's closed doors....
Mocked by the unfleshed critics,
Ridiculed by self believing, righteous idiots....

Liberal politicians, they got the job done,
JUST SOLDIERS..., accepted by none....
Unsung heroes, hung out to dry,
Misfits of society, they knew not why...

They served their country, with marked distinction,
Came home to witness, dignity's extinction....
They carried quietly, the scars of war,
Tolerated a society, erupted with putrid sores....

Enduring all, with a broken heart,
They carried on, tried to do their part....
Guilt was born, of shattered trusts and evil seeds,
Corrupting justice and their meritorious deeds....

Yet, they struggled, for what they believed,
On a daily basis, they were continually deceived...
Haunted by war and profound injustice,
Rejected society and its label of... maladjusted....

Can't help, JUST SOLDIERS, they are mentally ill,
It's their fault, they went off to kill....
But a sick society, much harder to treat,
Because, on its self, it continues to feast....

It persists to tell their soldiers, they are sick,
Counts its dollars, praises its rich....
Don't matter, JUST SOLDIERS, died by the score,
Too busy worshiping, Satan's great whore...!

They see a homeless veteran, kneel and pray,
Turn their heads, look the other way....
Much too busy, aborting babies, saving the seals,
Not their responsibility, to provide him with meals....

For you know, you are right,
To hell with they, who bore the fight....
Discard their bones, before they moulder,
After all, they are only, JUST SOLDIERS...!

The weight of my gear pulls on my shoulder straps,
Forty eight hours ago, we caught a brief nap ....
Sweat rolls down my face, burning my eyes,
Heavy fighting but, thank God, I'm still alive ....

Man, I'm totally exhausted, need a brief rest,
Just for a minute, need to catch my breath ....
No time to stop, the patrol must push on,
An urgent mission, nothing must go wrong ....

Dense triple canopy jungle, thick, green bamboo,
Damp, clammy fatigues,
stick to my flesh like they're glued....
I can smell the vegetation,
so earthy as it enters my nostrils,
Strange, extinct looking spiders and
centipedes scamper, like living fossils....

Our pointman signals, enemy trail watchers up ahead,
A silent knife attack, two khakied figures now lay dead..
Hardcore NVA, hope none of them got away,
If so, there could be hell to pay....

The trail branches off in several directions,
All leading up a great mountain, without exception ....
As we cautiously make our way,
We enter a large enemy base camp, to our dismay ... !

As my disbelieving eyes scan the terrain,
Adrenaline rushes to my brain ... !
Weapons switch from safety to full automatic,
To say we were violating an enemy battalion would be
diplomatic!

In boiling pots, rice is cooking,
I sense unseen eyes, at me, are glaring....
On a transistor radio, Vietnamese music is playing,
A silent prayer, I am praying....

No way, could this camp be seen from the air,
Not even sunlight
could penetrate this thick jungled lair...
Camouflaged bunkers,
spider holes and tunnels all over the place,
The enemy vanished, seemingly, without a trace... !

An underground hospital, surgically equipped,
Bamboo mats and stretchers filled every niche....
Bloody bandages strewn on the ground,
But even in here, not a soul was found....

please, remember me.....

"It's eerie, man, let's get the hell out of here,
Lets make like Charlie and disappear ... !"
We pass through the camp without incident,
Our trespass went unchallenged, no argument...

Instinct tells me, we should get well away from here,
Have an uncanny feeling,
"The Grim Reaper" be near ....
The past couple days we had the upper hand,
Had we now ventured too far
 into "Victor Charlie's" land ...?

We had located what we were looking for,
Hopefully undetected we'd sneak out the door....
Reporting what we had found,
We'd beat feet to safer ground....

There was no doubt we were on Charlie's turf,
Nearly undetectable punji pits were no quirk....
The thick jungle concealed many deadly snares,
Camouflaged bunkers easily reached by hidden stairs...

Stealthily we made our way,
Best to fight another day....
Silently, careful not to make a sound,
Swear I could hear my heart beat and pound....

My breathing labored as we climbed hill after hill,
The jungle so dense you couldn't see nihil....
Thick bamboo concealed a deadly enemy trap,
Blindly we had climbed right into their lap....

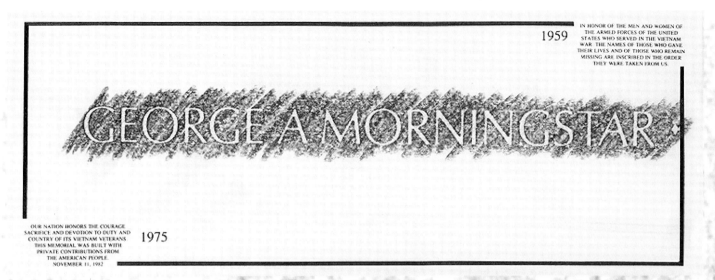

Murderous fire erupted nearly point blank,
A thunderous volley tore into our flank....
Machinegun bunkers to our front, AK's on our right,
Our whole column trapped in a vicious firefight...

Enemy soldiers in the banyans of trees,
Devastating fire, bringing us to our knees....
Hiding low amongst their roots,
The invisible enemy could safely shoot....

Our M-16's opened up with a deafening roar,
Through the bamboo our projectiles tore....
Pulling back we dove for cover,
Chicom grenades bounced one after the other...

In the kill zone I heard a friendly soldier's cries,
"Medic, medic! help me, or I'm going to die"...!
In the enemy's hate, they used him as bait,
To expose myself, they laid in wait....

Bullets whizzed by my head, three attempts to no avail,
They had him locked in an impenetrable jail....
For an eternity I heard him suffer and moan,
Then a single shot, he involuntarily let out
his final groan....

"Pull back, take the high ground to our rear!"
Firing like hell amid chaos and fear...
Three soldiers to my front fell to
a waiting machinegun,
The bastards had us on the run ... !

Thinking, "I'm only nineteen, I can not die!",
I heard myself scream as I fired so wild ....
Bamboo splinters tore into my flesh
Hot shrapnel stung, stealing my breath ...

Running obliquely down the hill,
Seemingly out of my body, as my blood was spilled...
I tripped and fell over a grotesque corpse
which had no face,
Death closing in, encompassing this hellish place ... !

Enemy soldiers block my path,
I fire again, a hail of bullets tear and slash....
I fall and roll farther down the hill,
Suddenly alone, all quiet and still....

Shocked, I quickly realize,
blood pumping from my chest,
I'm badly hurt, lungs gasping and rasping
to catch a breath....
I can't feel my legs, they will not move,
Please God, I don't want to die, too much to lose....

Weaker and weaker I become,
Blood is squirting from my lungs....
Enemy voices are all around me,
I'm partially hidden in tangled roots of bamboo trees....

I cover my body the best I can,
Scratching the moist ground with bloody hands....
The aroma of the musky earth,
once again fills my nose,
I can not resist as my eyes begin to close....

Slowly, quietly my strength fades away,
Making peace with The Almighty, I pray....
"Dear God, my country tis of thee,
All I ask is they PLEASE, REMEMBER ME ......

IN HONOR OF THE MEN AND WOMEN OF
THE ARMED FORCES OF THE UNITED
STATES WHO SERVED IN THE VIETNAM
WAR. THE NAMES OF THOSE WHO GAVE
THEIR LIVES AND OF THOSE WHO REMAIN
MISSING ARE INSCRIBED IN THE ORDER
THEY WERE TAKEN FROM US.

1959

OUR NATION HONORS THE COURAGE,
SACRIFICE AND DEVOTION TO DUTY AND
COUNTRY OF ITS VIETNAM VETERANS.
THIS MEMORIAL WAS BUILT WITH
PRIVATE CONTRIBUTIONS FROM
THE AMERICAN PEOPLE.
NOVEMBER 13, 1982

1975

NO LESS, DOES HE DESERVE!

"Soldier, soldier, where you been?"
Don't you know, you're needed again?
Building a monument, so deserved,
Your buddy's memory, help preserve...

Tis a big task, we're trying to do,
Need your help, to see it through....
Your airborne brothers, are working fast,
Making sure, the SPIRIT will last....

That AIRBORNE SPIRIT, you made renown,
To keep America, strong and sound....
Now, it's up to you, you see,
To help pass on, YOUR legacy...!

To those of you, whose soldier is gone,
In this effort, you so belong....
Our hearts, entwined with yours,
Tis his memory, we'll preserve...!

NO LESS, DOES HE DESERVE!

FORGET-ME-NOT

Death found us, on the battlefields of freedom,
Duty, Honor, Country, the noblest of reasons....
Fallen Screaming Eagles, we paid the toll,
Our sacrifices, etched, forever, on our souls....

Engaging battle, from the sky,
Looking death, straight in the eye....
We feared no enemy, on this earth,
On righteousness, Fallen Screaming Eagles perch...

Now we lie silent, in fields of green,
Our children, in FREEDOM, frolic in our dreams....
Eternal peace, granted, by a loving God,
Our highest decoration,
the FORGET-ME-NOT, to cover our sod....

MANY A YOUNG SOLDIER

Procreation, God's special gift of immortality,
Mortal man, lives on, by passing his seed....
By preservation of the species, death is defeated,
The fulfillment of life, is thus, completed....

When death precedes procreation,
It extinguishes life's rejuvenation....
One loses all, death, then final,
Of this, on earth, there can be, no denial....

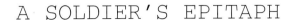

A SOLDIER'S EPITAPH

Grieve not for me,
For my spirit's
now free...
On wings of eagles,
I soar through
eternity...
Till the end of time,
With you, forever
I'll be....

MANY A YOUNG SOLDIER, has suffered this fate,
Left standing, alone, at eternity's gate....
Never tasting love, nor the fruits of its vine,
No children to follow, preserving him, in time....

He sacrificed all, for us, and liberty's flame,
Is there glow enough, to read his name...?
His wife and children, never begotten, to honor him,
We, his fellow soldiers, be amongst, his next of kin....

He was there, in every battle, our division ever fought,
Will his perpetuity, exist only, in the book of naught...
Tis up to us, to preserve his precious memory,
We must etch, in granite, his rendezvous with destiny....

AFTERGLOW

In early June of 1966 two battalions of the 101st Airborne Division were engaged in one of the most highly contested battles of the entire Viet Nam War. It was a slugfest, toe to toe, bitter, bloody fight, from beginning to end. Named "Operation Hawthorne", it unfolded in the triple canopy-jungled mountains in the central highlands near Dak To. Our mission was to relieve the besieged Special Forces camp at Toumorong that was being threatened by the crack North Vietnam-ese Army's 24th Infantry Regiment. Their mission was to draw in a U.S. Brigade and annihilate it, on their own well prepared turf and under their own terms.

Thirty two years have passed since those awful, bloody days of carnage and devastation. As a young PFC, nearing the end of my tour, I had no idea of the effect this battle would have on the rest of my life. For two and a half decades I struggled to keep the events of that time tucked neatly away, in the recesses of my mind. It was a wasted effort, for every day my mind was invaded by intrusive thoughts and flashbacks. My nights were no better, filled with restless, sleepless hours or un-wanted, dreaded nightmares.

During this twenty-five year period, I read nothing of the reports on this battle nor had I made contact with anyone who had fought there. I knew nothing of what had been documented or what had transpired in the lives of my fellow combatants. Then in 1989, I attended my first Army reunion. There I had the great honor and privilege to, once again, make contact with some very special people, the veterans of the 1st Brigade. This opened the door to several more reunions and of course, to many spirited and lively conversations. To my elation I found that all veterans, enlisted men,

NCO's, officers, and yes, even general officers were now interrelating, as if devoid of rank. It was and still is, a most thrilling and special occasion to talk to some people whom I used to (and still do) consider, next to God or at least God-like. Over time I discovered that I was even capable of carrying on conversations with them, in a relaxed manner; instead of just replying, "Yes Sir!" or "No Sir!"; while I snapped to "Attention"! Since 1989, I have enjoyed the company of these very special people, veterans of all ranks, at every available opportu-nity.

As my exposure to personal and written ac-counts of Dak To became more available, my curiosity and thirst for knowledge as to what actually happened there grew. I wanted to learn all I could about the battle. I wanted an overall view of the entire battle, not just the personal, narrow remembrances of my own limited experience. As a result I have read many old newspaper accounts, magazine articles, and several books. I visited the National Archives, read and copied official Army documents including maps, daily journals, battle logs and lessons learned.

After digesting all this, I have come to believe that the battles of Dak To, as recorded, are nearly as confusing in print as experiencing it at ground level as a PFC. This should not come as a surprise to anyone simply because of the very nature of the operation. It was extremely intense and complex because so many small units were engaged simultaneously throughout the area of operation. One thing does stand out clear and precise, it was a chaotic melee of heavyweight bouts, clear and simple!

Some of the material that I have addressed the decision making processes employed in this fierce and savage operation. Tactics and deployments have been questioned. I have even read where some people consider earned "glory and recognition" went to the wrong units or individuals. They are entitled to their opinions and conclusions whether reasonable or not. My purpose is to relate feelings from the heart and soul, not to second guess anyone or to be a "Monday Morning Quarterback".

Perhaps the most controversial incident to occur during Operation Hawthorne was the napalm drop. I have talked to several troopers of "C" company who were there. Some feel it was an overreaction, others feel that without it they wouldn't be here to discuss their feelings and thoughts on the subject. The majority opinion seems to go with the later. For a fact, many of the major players involved have little doubt that "C" company would have certainly died on that ridge without it. I know, some will say that I wasn't at "ground zero", and because of that fact, my conclusion is faulty and open to criticism, but the proof is written at the "bottom line". Yes, friendly as well as enemy casualties did result, but the drop did break off that enemy assault and allow time for "C" company to regroup and reorganize. The only credible, tangible evidence as to the success of this extraordinary decision is the results on that "bottom line" - SURVIVORS!

The other point of controversy that I noted was that Company "A" of the 1/327th Infantry, while attempting to rescue "C" company of the O'deuce, was the real enemy target, and that they bore the brunt of the fighting; without proper credit or recognition in the press. To me, this, whether true or not is irrelevant and does not matter for I know these soldiers are highly respected by their peers. Press recognition is nice but is not the ultimate acclaim. The only fact that really matters is that all our units were heavily engaged in bitter fighting and performed admirably. Our overall military mission was to seek out and destroy the enemy and personally..., to SURVIVE, not to worry about honorable mention. Some will ask, "How can I honestly and sincerely make this statement?" My answer is pure and simple, I, along with the rest of my weapons platoon, was attached to that company and faced that

enemy buzzsaw along with those very brave troops. This fact has never been mentioned in declassified print before and remains irrelevant to the history of that illustrious sister company of gallant warriors.

After studying all these accounts and considering the various facts, opinions and views contained therein, I have reached some basic conclusions. Amazingly, they are from the perspectives I had all along, before I did any research. They are from my own personal observations at dirt level as a PFC.

First and foremost, there is no doubt in my mind that every individual soldier engaged in Operation Hawthorne gave the upmost of himself for the successful completion of the mission. That every individual, no matter what rank, made the best possible decisions under the disjointed and confusing circumstances presented. Many hard and serious decisions had to be made without time for second guessing. I don't think there is a combat veteran alive that wouldn't admit that. We all have to live with our own decisions, made in combat, that had an effect on the lives of others. Undoubtedly, command decisions bore the greatest risk and responsibility. I thank God that He provided the great commanders and NCO's we had during those turbulent and deadly encounters.

I am still amazed by the extraordinary stamina displayed by our troops and cadre. To exhibit such strength and endurance under such terrible conditions and stress staggers the imagination. To fight so aggressively and bravely for such long periods of time without rest and basic sustenance is almost incomprehensible. Sleep deprivation seemed to have no negative effect on the ability of our soldiers or leaders. The heavy monsoon rains did not seem to dampen their spirits or abilities either. On the other hand, it certainly aided our enemies by providing cloud clover which restricted our medevacs, artillery, airstrikes and resupply of ammo and other much needed supplies. No doubt, they very cleverly took this into consideration before attempting to take on such a formidable opponent as the 1st Brigade.

Operation Hawthorne also offered me the

opportunity to observe, first hand, other magnificent units in action. The artillerymen at Toumorong who put up such a tenacious fight have left an indelible respect in my mind that will last forever. I will never forget those beehive rounds tearing into the enemy as they viciously charged their emplacements. The combat engineers fought bravely as infantrymen protecting the defensive perimeter from many concentrated attacks. Later they cut out landing zones with chainsaws under deadly enemy fire to extract our dead and wounded, with little concern for their own safety. The many aviation units as they risked all above the triple canopy jungles, under intense enemy fire, to provide the many services needed in support of the beleaguered ground troops. The Recondos as they stealthily made their way through the dense bamboo to provide much needed intelligence. The Tiger Force as they fearlessly took on an overwhelming superior enemy force at great risk and peril. All the units, all the men, God bless them all, "the long, the short and the tall" ......

The troopers of these individual units took on this well equipped, numerically superior enemy force, on their terms, on the well prepared ground of their choosing and under the protective cover of the monsoon season. Despite these many significant disadvantages they fought courageously and they prevailed. When it was all over the 24th NVA Regiment was rendered unfit as a fighting unit.

I have yet to meet a veteran of Dak To who has not been dramatically affected by what transpired there, all are humbled by the magnitude, dedication, unselfish efforts and sacrifices made there by our fellow soldiers. Many brave Screaming Eagles fell accomplishing this mission. Their efforts and sacrifices will never be forgotten. They are etched into the hearts, minds and souls of all who survived this ferocious battle.

Perhaps it truly is most fitting that the napalm drop be remembered as the single most significant event of Operation Hawthorne.... The explosive, searing, oxygen stealing, blasting inferno has long ago dissipated into oblivion, but in its wake it has left one brilliant incandescent legacy. This AFTERGLOW is the indomitable fighting Airborne spirit of the soldiers of the 1st Brigade, (separate) 101st Airborne Division, Viet Nam, 1965-68. I am most proud to be counted within your ranks, it is a great honor to have served with you. God bless you all.

Peter S. Griffin
Co. A, 2/502nd Infantry
1st Brigade (separate)
101st Airborne Division
Viet Nam, 1965-66

THOUGHTS, MEMORIES
AND TEARS

Thoughts expressed, written down on paper,
Not meant, to be chiseled, by the engraver....
Thoughts may differ, from man to man,
But shared, may cause, the joining of hands....

Memories, cherished remembrances, from our past,
Throughout our lives, meant to last....
Some, so happy, others, filled with sadness,
They surely fill, heart and soul, with tenderness....

Tears, formed by our sincere emotions,
Cleanse the soul, heart, and eyes....
Clearer we see, the reasons... why?
They cause us to grow, as the years go by....

THOUGHTS, MEMORIES, AND TEARS... form our feelings,
Feelings make us, such caring beings....
Without these, we could not bear the cost,
God created them, to understand and share what's lost...!

Feelings, certainly, the reasons why,
What causes man, to do or die....
They let us know, what's wrong, what's right,
They guide and bond us, throughout this life....

Feelings, shared, by you and I,
Together, made strong, as we live and die....
Binding us together, throughout our years,
I thank you for sharing,
THOUGHTS, MEMORIES, AND TEARS.

1959

IN HONOR OF THE MEN AND WOMEN OF
THE ARMED FORCES OF THE UNITED
STATES WHO SERVED IN THE VIETNAM
WAR. THE NAMES OF THOSE WHO GAVE
THEIR LIVES AND OF THOSE WHO REMAIN
MISSING ARE INSCRIBED IN THE ORDER
THEY WERE TAKEN FROM US.

OUR NATION HONORS THE COURAGE
SACRIFICE AND DEVOTION TO DUTY AND
COUNTRY OF ITS VIETNAM VETERANS.
THIS MEMORIAL WAS BUILT WITH
PRIVATE CONTRIBUTIONS FROM
THE AMERICAN PEOPLE.
NOVEMBER 11, 1982

1975

Photo/Art Credits

"WALL" TRACINGS:
David L. Dodson
George A. Morningstar
Melvin Reeder
Rudy Mantiad Sagon
Charles V. Turley

Challen K. Yee: cover, inside cover, 19, 24 25, 30, 35, 36, 37, 40, 43, 44, 45, 48, 52, 57, 58, 59, 82, 86, 88, 95, 98-99, 102-5, 110, 112-3, 132-3, 136, 142-143.
AUTHOR'S COLLECTION: 7, 8, 11-13, 22-23, 27, 38, 39, 51, 60a, 61, 62, 65-69, 74, 76, 81, 84, 100-1, 101, 108-9., 111, 114, 119-121, 122-3, 126-130, 134-5, 140-1, inside back cover, back cover.
> *Overleaf: The General J.M. Swing 11th Airborne Association color guard prepare for an Independence Day parade (1991), left to right: Bill Exline, Dale F. Yee, Bill Porteous, Manual Espinoza, Bob Hackl, Leroy Franklin, Ted Pezino, James B. King and his wife, Lorene.*

Index

Symbols

A

To ORDER
THOUGHTS, MEMORIES AND TEARS
copy this form

Quantity: _____ x 18.95 (U.S.) = $_____

Shipping/Handling: $5.00 per/destination $_____

               TOTAL = $_____

Enclosed is a check for the total amount shown above.
Please send my order to:

(Please print)

Name   _____

Address   _____

City   _____

State   _____ Zip Code _____

How did you find out about *Thoughts, Memories and Tears*?

_____

_____

_____

(Thank you for your order and any comments)

Make check payable to: Joye Enterprise
Send your order and payment to:

Joye Enterprise - Dept TMT
Box 60702, Palo Alto, CA. 94306-0702

Companies, professional groups, clubs, associations or other organizations
may qualify for special terms when ordering certain quantities of this title.
For information, write 'attn: Special Sales'